Adv~
Coach Yo~

"I know that *Coach Your Teen* ~~~~~~~~~~~~~~~ positive change to the lives of many pai ~~~~~ en. **This is the perfect resource for parents** who get that a 'new conversation' is absolutely necessary to support the growth of healthy individuals equipped to live 'full out and on-purpose.' May it be recognized as **a beacon of possibility for more peace, joy, and satisfaction for parents and teens everywhere!**" — Dr. Barbara Walton, Parent and President of the International Coach Federation

"Forget what you've heard about the teen years being the worst time of parenting. *Coach Your Teen to Success* offers tools to transform the relationship between teens and parents into a rewarding and fun time. This book is packed with **innovative and on-target advice**, exercises and tips to truly nurture and support teens to adulthood. **A must-read for anyone** who wants to parent more effectively and, more importantly, help teens become effective as adults. Why not give yourself and the special teen in your life the benefit of McRae's masterful, loving, affirming advice?" — Shannon Jackson Arnold, Parent and Author of *Everyone Loves Ice Cream*

"*Coach Your Teen to Success* makes you feel as if Barbara is speaking directly to you. The candid examples and insightful exercises at the end of each chapter demonstrate her wealth of knowledge in dealing with teens through her experiences as a mom, a Big Sister mentor, and a Master Certified Coach. With the dynamics of our younger generation ever changing, **it is critical that we**—the coaches, teachers, mentors, and parents learn how to **have more encouraging relationships**. We owe it to our future. This could be **one of the most important books you'll ever buy!**" — Robin Rogers, Parent and Executive Director, Big Brothers Big Sisters of Colorado, Inc. (Pikes Peak)

Also by Barbara McRae
*Less Drama, More Fun—Your Roadmap
to Personal Freedom*

C O A C H Your Teen to Success

7 Simple Steps

to Transform

Relationships

and Enrich Lives

By Barbara McRae, MCC
Founder of Teen Frontier
International

Achievers Trade Press
Powerful Ideas for Optimum Living

The intent of the author of this book is not to dispense medical advice or prescribe the use of any particular technique or treatment. This publication is designed to offer information of a general nature. It is sold with the understanding that the publisher is not engaged in rendering legal, psycho-therapeutic, or medical advice.

AUTHOR'S NOTE: To preserve the confidentiality of the coaching relationship, pseudonyms have been used and certain characteristics have been disguised in the case histories recounted.

A portion of the profits from this book will be donated to Big Brothers Big Sisters of Colorado, Inc. BBBS is the preeminent youth mentoring organization in the US. For 100 years, BBBS has helped children reach their potential through professionally supported, one-to-one relationships and a program with proven and measurable impact. For more information, call 303-433-6002 or visit www.bbbscolo.org.

Requests for permission or information about bulk orders should be addressed to Achievers Trade Press, 10 Boulder Crescent, Suite 300A, Colorado Springs, CO., 80903. 888-409-5433.

Special thanks from Teen Frontier International to the staff at the Jenkins Group, Inc. for their guidance during the book design and production process.

Published by Achievers Trade Press
10 Boulder Crescent, Suite 300A
Colorado Springs, CO 80903

Publisher's Cataloguing-in-Publication Data
McRae, Barbara.

Coach your teen to success : 7 simple steps to transform relationships and enrich lives / by Barbara McRae. — Colorado Springs, CO : Achievers Trade Press, 2004.

p. ; cm.
ISBN: 0-9759861-0-4

1. Success in adolescence. 2. Parent and teenager. 3. Self actualization (Psychology) in adolescence. 4. Adolescent psychology. I. Title.

BF724.3.S9 M37 2004   2004110489
158.1/083/5—dc22   CIP

Book production and coordination by Jenkins Group, Inc. • www.bookpublishing.com

Interior production by Debra M. Beck/Beck Designs
Cover design by Kelli Leader

Printed in the United States of America
08 07 06 05 • 6 5 4 3 2

DEDICATION

To the wonderful new teenagers, our future leaders, and to the wise adults who bring out their best.

ACKNOWLEDGMENTS
(and appreciation) for:

Katherine R. McRae—daughter and friend. Having you in my life is a privilege and a pleasure; you'll always remain in my heart.

Richard C. Sandquist—loving husband, best friend, and my biggest fan. Thanks for contributing a father's perspective to this material. I love you!

Erin J. Slusher—volunteer proofreader, children's songwriter, and brainstorming buddy. Thank you for your cheerleading and for all of your offers to help.

Robert H. Snyder—editor extraordinaire and former step family newspaper columnist. Thank you for your passion and endorsements.

Tsen Tsing—grand teacher, dear friend, and my highest inspiration. Once again, this book would not have been written without your support. A world of thanks!

The Creator—supreme divinity from whom all blessings and creativity abundantly flow. Thank you for your eternal love.

And heartfelt thanks to all of my wonderful clients (adults, preteens, and teens) who have either directly or indirectly contributed to this book.

CONTENTS

APPENDICES

When a man and a woman decide to have a child, they are filled with hopes and dreams of how beautiful, sensitive, and clever their child will be. These dreams provide the parents with a principled way of deciding how to support and promote certain kinds of behavior in their infant, child, and young adult. The wise parent soon discovers the limits of the influence s/he can and should exercise on offspring, and thereby learns to appreciate the unique qualities of the mature human being s/he was instrumental in developing.

John Grinder
co-founder of Neurolinguistic Programming (NLP),
quoted by Genie Laborde in *Influencing with Integrity*,
Syntony Publishing, 1994

PROLOGUE

I am passionate about positively impacting teens, our future leaders. There exist many good-hearted people who want their teens to succeed and to have productive and satisfying lives, but these parents don't have the tools or the skills to help with challenges that they themselves are often still secretly struggling with. We can only teach what we already know. Sometimes it's clear that ingrained strategies work; sometimes it's not. More often than not, when adults feel defeated, they tighten their grip, and this leads to further alienation. It doesn't have to be this way. You can learn to give your teen what he or she needs while maturing.

Think back to when your child was young and completely dependent on you for all physical needs. Once the child was in grade school, the two of you still experienced a strong connection, but a transition took place. The child began to mentally absorb information independently from you. In the preteen stage, your child increasingly makes more of his or her own choices. What happens to your role during these different stages of your child's development? Are you evolving with your child? Are you still a caretaker, policing everything?

The universal experience of teens transitioning into adulthood marks a time of profound adjustment for both parent and child. At this confusing stage, it is natural for kids to test their limits as they express their need for independence. Just as the "terrible twos" triggered the child's need for physical independence, the onset of puberty triggers emotional and mental independence, heightening parent-child conflict. The confusion and frustration parents feel diminishes when they know what to expect and when they have effective strategies for lovingly guiding teens during this critical stage of development.

A feeling of invincibility—often hormone or stimulant induced—that accompanies a teenager's quest for independence is considered a top factor in the number-one killer of young motorists in the United States today. According to Amisafe.net, automobile accidents are the leading cause of death for children ages 15-19. Statistics show that although teenagers account for just seven percent of the driving population, they are involved in 14 percent of all accidents and deaths. One out of three teens is involved in a crash during their first year of driving. In 1999 alone, there were over 2,000,000 teen driving crashes and 6,000 deaths (www.amisafe.net, 2003).

On the other hand, another area of concern to parents, educators, and mental health professionals is the rise in teen suicides; it has tripled in the last 25 years! According to the current posting on the American Academy of Child and Adolescent Psychiatry's web site, suicide among young people continues to increase dramatically. Teen suicide is considered the second or third leading cause of death for 15-to-24-year-olds, even though it is seriously underreported (www.aacap.org, 2004). See Appendix 1 for Teen Suicide Prevention.

We are experiencing an age of high-anxiety parenting. Adults and teens are at a critical fork in the road. Which path will you choose? Will you continue using outdated parenting approaches regardless of the breathtaking changes we are all experiencing in our lives, or will you take into account the unique needs and opportunities of today's teenager?

In my view, if we don't revisit many of the parenting beliefs that were passed down to us from our own parents, we will continue to see increased anguish, teen violence, drug addiction, and suicides. Kids are crying out for help in very dramatic ways. As a result of my work with teens, individuals, and organizations, I know firsthand that the old command-and-control model stifles the human spirit and invariably produces conflict, whether it's in the office, at school, or at home. The opposite approach of *laissez-faire* (or hands-off) parenting, isn't the answer, either. Young adults need the gift of guidance. They need adults to take the time and have the courage to lovingly identify and enforce appropriate boundaries with reasonable consequences.

As a certified personal coach, I have participated in and witnessed phenomenal transformations in the workplace due to enlightened leadership. An important shift is taking place, with leaders now inspiring others to go beyond developing competencies and skills to growing in the areas of integrity, character, and personal development. My clients and I now realize that this new whole-person approach to success is just as relevant for guiding teens into well-rounded, contributing members of society as it is for adults.

I have a vision. I see parents (and other adults who interact with teens) dropping their assumptions about teens and replacing traditional roles with new methods that are grounded in modern scientific research. I see parents and teachers embracing the new role of coach and guide to help teens, our leaders of tomorrow, develop into resourceful, responsible, and empathic adults. Using this approach, parents would see their children as wise souls in young bodies, not empty vessels. And adults could focus on what they can learn from their kids, not just what teens can learn from adults. Imagine teens and parents expressing themselves authentically in a loving way. Adults would no longer feel stressed and frustrated with teens, and teens would desire and appreciate adult input in making their life choices. I see a new world where kids are provided a safe environment to develop and are treated with great honor and respect, both at home and in the classroom.

How would it feel, if as a parent coach, you could offer the following I AM statements to your teen?

I am your mentor in helping you become the person who is waiting to emerge.

I am your champion when you feel discouraged and misunderstood.

I am your sounding board when you make important choices.

I am your teacher in helping you learn to think and apply knowledge.

I am your beacon to light the way when you are confused.

I am your unconditional support when you slip and fall.

I am your role model in demonstrating effective communication and life skills.

I am your partner in helping you take action to reach goals that are important to you.

My purpose in writing this book is to help parents—and anyone working with teens—to become valuable influencers, guiding teens to their highest potential. Using proven modern parent-teen coaching techniques that have already benefited so many parents, you will successfully create a teen-friendly environment that contributes to experiencing positive, harmonious relationships. As an experienced Big Sister and an active board member of Big Brothers Big Sisters of Colorado, Inc., I am dedicated to mentoring present day preteens and teens.

The information in this book draws on my 20 years of experience in training adults in advanced communication techniques, personally parenting and mentoring three teenagers into adulthood, and my work as a pioneer in comprehensive parent coaching methods. As my clients learned to enhance their personal and professional relationships, these adults sought my help to better relate to and guide their children, especially during the troublesome teen years. Soon it became apparent that there is a need for cutting-edge techniques, effective support, and solid parent advice for raising contemporary teens.

Contained in this book are *seven simple tools* that you can apply immediately to help you develop powerful communication and relating skills for reconnecting with teens. Wouldn't it be great to know how to provide your teen with the best preparation for adulthood? The emphasis in this book is on implementation. Every technique I share with you has been thoroughly tested and honed to give you optimum results, as long as you apply them consistently. May you be filled with...

- Peace of mind that you are doing your best as a parent
- Joy in having a healthy close relationship with your teen, and
- Satisfaction in knowing that you are contributing greatly in leaving a legacy for our future.

PART ONE

Setting the Coaching Foundation

CHAPTER 1

What Parents Want

Welcome to *Coach Your Teen To Success*. Whether you are a parent or an adult interacting with contemporary teens, imagine

- Confidently supporting your teen into adulthood
- Collaborative communications that cause you to hear and be heard
- Discovering simple coaching strategies that optimize any situation

Yes, it is possible to enjoy open and stimulating high-functioning relationships with teens during these potentially turbulent years. In working with parents across the nation, Canada and in Europe, I discovered what parents want most from their teens. Let's begin our parent-teen coaching journey together by reviewing the top seven *wants* outlined in this chapter.

1. Teens to understand that they care.

   For a parent, there is much to be concerned about: drug use, drinking while driving, suicide, violence, and so on. Parents care, even if they don't always know how to show it. They make rules and want kids to cooperate, because they want their kids to be okay.

2. To know what's going on in their teens' life.

   Parents worry about their teens' safety and want to be in the communication loop to know that they are all right. Parents would prefer it if teens would be open and honest and talk about what they are experiencing and feeling. They want to be involved without having to always be the ones to ask. They want to feel part of their kids' lives.

3. Teens to realize that they are human, too.

   Parents want their kids to appreciate the things they do to help them and for their kids to let go of the mistakes their parents have made. Teens don't come with instructions; parents learn as they go.

4. Their kids to understand their values.

   It's important to parents to pass their values on to their offspring and have them understand the benefits of living according to your values. (Some parents want to have their kids take on all of the parents' values without discovering their own; however, most parents are open to discussing values.)

5. To be heard and to have their opinions acknowledged.

   Parents don't enjoy nagging or one-sided conversations any more than teenagers do. They would like to know that their communications are received and given consideration.

6. To be treated with respect.

   Effective communication can only happen when each party has respect for the other. Respect doesn't mean that there must be agreement. It means that each person has the opportunity to openly share his or her point of view and to listen to the other's, without always having to be right.

7. Teens to ask for help when facing problems.

   Parents like to be asked for their opinions and to be useful in sorting out all of the options teens regularly face. It can be a joint process.

Can you relate to this list? Is there anything else that you want, as a parent (grandparent, teacher, mentor, and so on)? Take a moment and jot it down below.

_____

_____

_____

Excellent! Now let's have you describe, in detail, what your desired communication and relationship with your teen looks like. When was the last time you felt close to your child (or to an adult)? Was it easy to communicate in that environment? Did you enjoy being with this person? What factors do you think contributed to being in rapport? See yourself as someone who has all the resources to have a harmonious relationship with your teen right now. Ask yourself how you want to relate to him or her.

What if you didn't come from a family that exhibited healthy communication and relating styles and you are having trouble visualizing what your ideal situation would look like? Simply remind yourself of other masterful relationship-builders (at the office, on TV, in the movies) you have experienced or observed. Picture these persons in your mind. What were their behaviors? How did others respond to them? Which qualities would you want for yourself? Now go back and complete the exercise.

Next, describe your current biggest frustrations with your teen.

List your concerns and fears.

_____

_____

_____

_____

_____

_____

Now identify the three most important changes you'd like to see in how you and your teen are relating to each other.

1 _____

2 _____

3 _____

Think about the strategies you have employed in trying to influence change. What have you tried that you now know does not work?

_____

_____

_____

_____

Great! Now, we know what not to do. Are you ready to wipe the slate clean and learn a new approach? Let's find out.

If you haven't taken the time to answer the questions above, go back and do it now. If you are reading this material at home without the benefit of participating in a workshop or having a coach at your side to help guide you, you may be tempted to skip this part and the other exercises throughout this book. Please don't. You may be thinking that these steps don't really matter, that you're too busy, or that you'll do them later. I urge you to reconsider. Research supports enhanced learning through taking the time to think through these exercises and committing your thoughts to paper.

My experience is that readers and clients who are fully committed to their goals are willing to do what is necessary to achieve results; they don't skip steps. Consequently, their results are accelerated and are ten times more profound. In athletic performance and competition, one of the coaching methods involved is for the coach to provide drills to enhance the skills of the players. Without a coach, most athletes would not be able to attain the same heights (except perhaps young Michael Jordan, who was known to go back to the gym to continue the drills on his own, after practice). What I want is for you to get as much out of this program as possible—for you to exceed your own expectations.

A person who reads this book without doing the exercises is like a skier choosing to trek up the mountain instead of taking the ski lift. Without the lift, much energy and time is wasted. With the benefit of the lift, the skier reaches the top quickly, has many more opportunities to experiment with new runs, and can enjoy new experiences at the top. Enough said. Let's continue by looking at what your teenager wants from you.

CHAPTER 2

What Teenagers Want from Their Parents

1. For parents to be willing to understand what it's like being a teen today.

   Most parents can remember their teenage years and think that they therefore understand everything that a contemporary teen is facing. Although you, too, experienced adolescence, you lived in a different time, with fewer choices and less freedom. Transitioning from child to grown-up is a personal journey. Don't assume that you know what it's like for your teen; ask and listen. You won't always understand, but that's okay. Be supportive. Teens that have a good relationship with their parents have a huge advantage in growing up.

2. For parents to realize that it's important for teens to have opportunities to practice making their own decisions.

   Teens need to make up their own minds about things, and parents generally want to save their kids from making mistakes. Your own parents did exactly the same thing, with limited results. There are no real mistakes, just opportunities for feedback. The earlier our kids learn about consequences from making their own choices—when the stakes are lower—the less likely it is that they will get into serious trouble. Offer guidance; stay away from mandates unless it's absolutely necessary. If everything is a mandate, you lose your influence. Keep the communication lines open; teens want guidance and support.

3. For parents to participate in and stay involved in their lives.

   Teens want you to be interested in their lives without taking over. Ask questions without turning conversations into interrogations. Respect their privacy, but don't withdraw completely. Be there; adjust your style to the situation. As a child strives for self-identity there will naturally exist a push and pull between parent and teen. Young teens are in an in-between place. They're not children and not yet adults. This can be confusing for both kids and parents. If you use the same parenting methods that you did when your teen was a child, you will no longer experience the same results. Schedule time with your teen and talk to him or her about personal interests. Spend time together doing what your teen enjoys. Keep the connection alive.

4. For parents to show consideration for them and respect them.

   Teens, like most individuals, want parents to respect their views, even if their parents don't agree with them. Face it, we all want to be loved and accepted for who we are.

We all belong to the family of human beings. Was there an adult in your life that you opened up to, someone special who didn't judge you? Do you want to be that someone for your kid? Realize that you can acknowledge another viewpoint without making it right or wrong. Another's viewpoint is just as important as your own. It's natural and necessary for teenagers to question, explore, and experiment as they search for their true identities as individuals. Experimentation helps teens mature into adults, and it doesn't have to be uncomfortable or dangerous.

5. For parents to be trustworthy and demonstrate integrity.

    Parents are powerful role models. Kids will act out in their teens the behaviors that they observed in their caretakers during childhood. The traditional request to "do as I say and not as I do" is defunct. It didn't work well in the past, and it won't work now. Help your teen understand the reasoning behind your requests. Make sure your rules are reasonable, and be consistent. Watch your promises to and agreements with your teen. If you tell your preteen that at age 18 he or she will no longer have a curfew, don't change that agreement on your teen's 18th birthday! Set good standards for yourself so that you can embody those for your teen.

6. For parents to give their advice and opinions when asked for them.

    Have you noticed what happens when you give your view without checking to see if it's wanted? Does any of it sink in? Not likely. When your communication becomes a one-sided lecture, it usually gets tuned out. Create an opening for your message to be received. Ask your teen, "Would it be okay to share my views?" Parents are always amazed at how well asking for permission works if it's done sincerely. If your teen doesn't want your opinion and says so, respect that and keep silent. Timing is everything! You can ask again at another time when he or she is feeling more receptive. Remember, force-feeding your message creates further separation, not a closer connection. Most teens will want to continue communicating with you if they feel that they have a choice in the matter.

7. For parents to understand that the teen's friends are important.

Your teen's friends are just as important to him or her as your friends are to you. Friends are often in the same position or emotional space as your teen, and this creates a bond. Be supportive of your teen in this area; we each have different social needs. One of my clients didn't realize at first that her son needed social interaction as much as she requires time to herself. Some parents feel threatened by their teenagers' friends. They think that these friends have more influence over their kids than they do. Friends may have influence on teens' choices with respect to some short-term issues (clothes, dating, and so on), but teen surveys have reported that parents have more influence on choices concerning long-term issues such as whether to attend college, or job and career plans. Parents are still major influencers when it comes to a teen's character and level of integrity.

8. For parents to stay connected with them so that they can feel their parents' love.

Most of us know about the importance of bonding with a young child to ensure healthy emotional development; a young child needs a great deal of physical closeness. Teens need to feel a close bond or connection with their parents, too. In this developmental stage, the connecting power comes from empathic communication. According to Daniel Goleman's groundbreaking work on "emotional intelligence," empathy is the basis for positively relating to others. A lack of parental empathy negatively impacts an adolescent's development. Generally, the more a parent can demonstrate empathy with a teen, the stronger their relationship will be, and the more the teen will be able to empathize with others.

The above list was compiled based on material gathered by interviews I conducted with teenagers, parents, and teachers. It is by no means a complete list, just the highlights. Be sure to ask your teen what he or she needs and wants from you.

Exercise

In reviewing what you want and what your teen wants from you, what have you noticed about what you both have in common? Take a moment to write down your thoughts.

_____

_____

_____

_____

_____

_____

The remaining chapters outline a step-by-step approach for effectively reconnecting to your teen and building a strong foundation to more successfully guide your teen in all areas of life.

CHAPTER 3

Parent Coach Evolution

L ike it or not, we aren't living in the same world we did even a few years ago. Yesterday's influencing and parenting skills no longer bring success with the teens of today and tomorrow. I know our parents may have felt this way, too, but the children of today are displaying a set of unique characteristics. Here is a summary of the 10 predominant new behavior traits found in children born since the mid-80s:

1. They have short attention spans and get distracted easily.

2. They have lots of physical energy (prone to hyperactivity).

3. They are highly sensitive people with empathy and compassion.

4. They have a great need for attention and quality time.

5. They resist absolute authority (without a dialogue and choice).

6. They are strong-willed and cannot be forced to do anything.

7. They have trouble bonding with others who are unlike themselves.

8. They are frustrated with the status quo and look for a better way.

9. They speak with conviction and will ask for what they want.

10. They sense hidden feelings and can get very angry when they feel insincerity or disrespect.

Do you recognize any of these traits? Some of these behaviors also resemble symptoms that indicate Attention Deficit Disorder (ADD)/Attention Deficit Hyperactivity Disorder (ADHD). If you think that your child could fall into this category, please investigate this thoroughly before using this label. In a study conducted by Dr. Leonard Sax where he reported that "...the initial diagnosis of ADD came from teachers in more than half of the cases, from parents in 25% of cases and from the primary physician in 10%; the rest of the time ADD was identified by a psychologist, neighbor or friend" (www.healthyplace.com, 2003). It is estimated that nearly three million children in the United States use Ritalin to cope with ADD/ADHD. Some claim that we have become a "Ritalin Nation" and that there is a danger of misdiagnosis (i.e., hyperactivity can also be the result of poor nutrition or deep sadness, feeling misunderstood and unwanted).

Go to Appendix 2 for additional helpful information and resources.

Given the above mentioned factors and the prescription drug epidemic, to succeed you need a fundamentally different way of approaching modern teens, a way of creating mutually supportive, high-trust relationships that transcend the traditional parent-child roles. Dr. Breggin reports that children and teenagers quickly improve their behavior and outlook when adults provide them with a better environment. Parenting that resorts to controlling or manipulating when the going gets tough causes destructive interactions. Coaching creates positive interactions, because its premise is that humans are good; they have intrinsic worth and warrant honor and respect just as they are. What would happen if you were willing to see teens as creative and lovable individuals instead of a group to be avoided, tolerated, or feared?

One thing is certain. Everything is changing and will continue to change at a rapid pace. A significant factor leading our cultural changes is our highly advanced technology. Parents of contemporary teens grew up with a basic telephone, radio, and a handful of channels on network television. Young people of today use cell phones, watch hundreds of stations on cable or satellite TV, cruise the Internet, use laptop computers, spend hours swapping Instant Messages, and listen to CDs. The way in which we gather, receive, and communicate information has shifted. Thanks to the Internet, modern teens have an abundance of knowledge instantly available to them. I've seen 3-year-olds who are significantly more computer literate than their parents! Our technological explosion strongly impacts every aspect of our lives, including parenting teens. In many ways, teens today are more advanced and savvy than those of previous generations.

It's no longer business as usual; parenting as usual won't develop teens into fully functioning, confident, productive adults. Teens don't come with directions, but if they did, the directions would be obsolete by now.

Have you noticed that the old fear-based parenting methods we experienced in the 1950s and early 1960s don't work? Guilt tactics, threats, condescension, and other old forms of discipline are defunct. It's like using a rotary phone instead of a cell phone with video imaging. This begs the question, "What are you, as a parent, willing to do to evolve yourself?"

In business, the role of the manager is evolving to one of leader, coach, and facilitator—with good reason. The old command-and-control military model of managing has serious drawbacks, except in emergency situations. Used indiscriminately, it mostly disempowers employees, limiting initiative and creativity. When capable employees constantly need to wait for further instructions from a manager to proceed, dependency and inefficiencies result. Research has shown that a participative style of leadership generally yields better long-term results, particularly for organizations that require employees with higher skill levels. The new style of leadership inspires change without using strict authority.

The best approach is one that uses situational awareness, that is, fully understanding what needs to be accomplished in a given context. When your children are very young and are dependent on you for all of their needs, then the old parenting technique (expecting children to do as you say with little discussion) makes sense. Telling your five-year-old, "Be sure to look both ways before crossing the street" is good parenting. At age ten, however, a child no longer needs that particular reminder. This kind of communication is considered a mismatch. In this example, the parent is not taking into account the current development level of the child. Thus, frustration and potential conflict is likely to result.

To put it another way: if, as a leader, you find yourself in a burning building, your priority is to help everyone escape quickly by telling others clearly what they need to do. It would not be appropriate to facilitate a discussion in which everyone has their say. After the fire, when your goal is to reconstruct, the wise leader invites others to contribute their ideas, listens to everyone's point of view, and sincerely considers all viewpoints prior to making a final decision. A good leader builds strong relationships and develops his or her staff into highly functioning contributors. Hence, progressive organizations are choosing to move from traditional management toward collaborative leadership with a coaching mentality. The following chart shows what that entails.

EVOLUTION IN BUSINESS

From Managing	To Leading
Directs (issues orders)	Coaches, facilitates
Demands respect	Shows respect
Limits	Empowers
Harps on weaknesses	Builds on strengths
Follows military archetype	Uses teaching archetype
Knows all the answers	Asks powerful questions

The same shift is beginning to take place in the family unit (and in the classroom), as the next chart demonstrates.

EVOLUTION IN TEEN PARENTING

From Traditional Parenting	To Enlightened Coaching
Telling	Powerful questioning
Directing	Guiding
Controlling	Role modeling
Demanding respect	Showing respect
Decision making	Facilitating
Limiting	Empowering

Enlightened coaching relies on advanced communication and enhanced relating to foster confident, emotionally balanced, responsible, and motivated young adults. Coaching serves as the universal connector in successful relationships in any context (workplace, sports field, schoolroom, or home). Bob Nardelli, CEO of Home Depot, believes that unless coached, people will never reach their maximum capabilities. Modern coaching is about 20 years old and blends the best of sports coaching and professional consulting. It has been featured in well over 100 major media outlets, including TV, radio, newspapers, magazines, and so on—due to the extraordinary high regard professional coaches display toward honoring and developing their clients' existing inner resources.

Think about it, if executives, Olympic athletes, and top performers can benefit from modern coaching, why not you and your teen? Imagine using your enlightened approach to uplift and model healthy, collaborative interactions for your children. Left to our own devices, we often treat our kids the way we were treated. Have you ever found yourself saying things to your offspring that you vowed you'd never say to YOUR child? Of course, you have. We all have. With enlightened parent-teen coaching skills, you will give your teens the gift of unconditional support, bringing out their best.

A Parent Coach is someone who ...

- helps teens develop more rapidly for a brighter future
- tailors communication and listening skills to the individual needs of the teen
- engages in an on-going respectful partnership that produces fulfilling results
- contributes observations and questions, creating clarity and moves the teen toward productive action
- helps teens build on their natural strengths
- believes that teens are creative and resourceful
- accepts and protects the inherent vulnerability of each teen
- looks at how all the parts of a teen's life work together
- maintains objectivity in the best interest of the teen, the community, and society

- understands that the power of coaching comes from the synergy created between coach and teen.

Sounds lovely, doesn't it? Think back to when you were a teenager. Did you have someone in your life that treated you with the utmost honor and respect? If not, you probably wish you had. It IS possible to give the gift of loving and respectful guidance right now, balancing parental authority with empathy. The earlier you start practicing with the tools I will be sharing with you, the faster you will realize your new relationship with your teen.

Exercise

A How could your teen benefit from you becoming a parent coach? List 5-10 compelling reasons.

1. _____

2. _____

3. _____

4. _____

5. _____

6. _____

7. _____

8. _____

9. _____

10. _____

Once you consistently listen intently to young people, let them know that their views matter, and appreciate their unique qualities and opinions then the possibilities for benefits are endless.

B Now write down your purpose for being willing to become a parent coach. Clearly state your promise to yourself here:

_____

_____

_____

_____

If you don't capture your commitment on paper and refer to it often, it's easy to forget it or get derailed. Your commitment is also one of the strongest aids you have to outfox any Yeahbuts that may surface now or along this new path you are taking. (Refer to the next chapter for more details.)

C How will you know if you have achieved your vision of being a parent coach? What will be different? How will it feel?

_____

_____

_____

_____

_____

Having your vision clearly defined, fuels your motivation to act with confidence going forward. If you feel that you already have good strategies for building great relationships with teens, you can always make it even better. If you feel that the gap between where you are and where you need to go is too wide, don't give up. Keep reading.

SPECIAL OFFER: Email your request for free tips on how to create a compelling vision by contacting us through www.teenfrontier.com.

"The earlier someone is taught how to live the most effortless, harmonious, and creative way, the more likely it is that all of life will bring success. This is what we are asked to pass on to our children, and if we can do it, nothing brings more joy and pride."

Deepak Chopra, M.D.

CHAPTER 4

Outfox the Yeahbuts

Have you noticed that the bigger the change seems, the stronger the attack of Yeahbuts get? Expect them to show up for you; they're normal. The Yeahbuts role is to defend who you've been and what you've done in the past. Know that as a human being, Yeahbuts are part of your survival operating system, leftover from when humans lived in caves. In some ways this protective system still contributes to your physical safety, but mostly it stops you from making new choices. Yeahbuts sound like they are coming from you, but don't make the mistake into thinking that they are you; they're not—no matter how convincing and persistent they sound.

Let's say that you are a chocoholic who realizes that if you want to feel better and keep your face from breaking out that you had better eliminate (or severely reduce) your chocolate intake. You savor one more piece of Godiva chocolate and get rid of the box. The next day at the office it's a co-workers birthday and the entire department is celebrating with a luscious death-by-chocolate cake. Someone hands you a piece of cake and in your mind you hear, "Why not just have a little piece? It won't hurt. I can start the 'no more chocolate plan' tomorrow." You succumb to the cajoling voice of your Yeahbut and break your commitment to yourself. When the notion of commitment—a pledge to do something specific—shows up, more Yeahbuts often join in to keep you stuck. "If only I were more disciplined." Or, "I've always had a problem with commitment." Or, "It's just too difficult for me."

Believing that you have a bigger problem with commitment than the rest of us is part of the problem. There is nothing wrong with you. Once you realize that Yeahbuts are merely old pre-recorded messages, you can takeover your own show. Yeahbuts play in your head and are activated like your prerecorded voice mail greeting. If you give in to these old messages, they can run your life. Take back your power and your freedom to choose; hit the delete button and rerecord a message that is in support of your desired goal, such as, "I no longer choose to experience the uncomfortable aftermath of eating chocolate, of smoking, or of controlling the conversation" or whatever the case may be. Below you'll find effective ways to help you be more resourceful in outfoxing your Yeahbuts.

Encourage your Yeahbuts to reveal themselves and speak up; don't suppress them or they'll turn into snipers.

- Be aware that you are not your thoughts or your feelings; let the Yeahbuts pass through you

- Acknowledge them; say "I hear you," but don't engage in battle; it will be too exhausting

- Keep a Yeahbuts log; then when they repeat, you can be amused and say to yourself, "Here comes number seven."

- Find an antidote; if you don't have one because your Yeahbuts are outside of your locus of control, hear them as words playing on a radio and switch stations

■ Remind yourself of your pledge and visualize your ideal outcome

■ Develop a support network of friends who are willing to help you change; not the ones who keep the status quo intact

■ Work with a professional coach or coaching buddy who has already successfully mastered Yeahbuts in his or her life.

Exercise

Think about a change you are considering and write down your Yeahbuts below. Then use the above methods to outfox your Yeahbuts to get free. Use the chart below. The first two examples are there to guide you.

Log Yeahbut	List Strategy for Yeahbut	Take Action
1. "I've never been good at this."	Acknowledge your self-limiting thought and remind yourself that you can learn.	Place your focus on the benefits of your new pledge.
2. "What if I make matters worse?"	Acknowledge the fear of failing and face the fear with courage by moving forward anyway.	Keep reading and practice often.

Log Yeahbut	List Strategy for Yeahbut	Take Action

Clients report that often by simply capturing the Yeahbuts on paper and naming them, they lose their stronghold. Don't be tempted to just refute them "in your head." When you engage with Yeahbuts, they win. After you have created the above log, you can objectively ACKNOWLEDGE them mentally more easily.

CHAPTER 5

The Six Stages of Change

As mentioned in the previous chapter, initially you may feel some resistance in forging a new future, in allowing your role to change as your children develop. This is natural. Keep the big picture in mind as you practice your new skills. It has been said that the wise leave the road and find the way; fools cling to the way and lose the road. The changes that take place as your kids grow are unavoidable; all parents face them. If you want to be a valuable coach to your teen, you must be willing to make adjustments to your parenting style.

Know that behavior follows self-image. This understanding is critical for making any desired changes. If you see yourself as someone who has difficulty changing, this then becomes your self-fulfilling prophecy. To ready yourself for change, see yourself as a person who has already mastered the change.

The reasons that change seems so difficult for many of us are found in the six predictable stages of change. If you don't know what the stages are, you will be less equipped to move through them easily. For some, these stages are transparent. For others, fear can get triggered and block the natural process of change. That's when many people give up; ironically, often they quit just prior to experiencing their most profound breakthroughs.

1. Loss of focus: This stage corresponds to the initial realization that change may be necessary or beneficial. Most people experience this as being overwhelmed. There is fuzziness of thought and maybe even a sense of paralysis. You feel as though your mind is temporarily short-circuiting, or it intermittently goes blank.

A mother feeling the strain of being ignored by her teenage son (who was away at college) came to me for help. Following a family argument that had occurred during the holidays, he wasn't returning her phone calls or responding to any of her attempts to communicate. Joan realized that her approach tended to be heavy-handed and that her demands for a close relationship with her 19-year-old were getting in the way of her having any kind of relationship at all with him. She was tearfully sad, and her thinking was muddy.

2. Denial and delay: Next, the mind defends against the change by denying that anything needs to change, that anything has really changed, or that anything is going to actually change. Denial is resistance that appears to protect you from the impact of change. You may be tempted to change the subject or to get up and leave, if you're discussing the need for change with another person. When you're alone, signs of denial include a mental reluctance to dwell on thoughts of needed change.

What Joan really wanted was to return to the past, to have her son be receptive to her mothering again. Due to the safe environment that Joan and I created to help her shift her role from parent to parent coach, she was willing to feel and articulate her resistance to change. She also became aware that she felt threatened and replaced by her son's girlfriend. Denial can last for a few seconds, a few days or months, or even for much longer. In this case, within one coaching session, Joan was able to refocus on how the present situation could benefit her, how it could contribute to learning more about herself, and how she could step into being a better role model.

3. Creative tension: You have committed to the change and are now in transition. There is a gap between the old (past, ingrained behavior patterns) and the new (preferred behaviors). This is the creative tension stage. It feels chaotic and unsettling. It's like remodeling your home: the necessary dismantling process can be messy and unpleasant. Uncertainty may settle in as well, because the desired results are nowhere in sight yet. Clarity arises out of confusion. Acknowledge any discomfort that you are feeling and keep true to your vision, your preferred outcome.

Joan was committed to redefining her relationship with her teen, and as she did, more insights surfaced for her about what she wanted her enhanced relationship to look like. She was eager to work toward her goals; yet, during this process, she found herself doubting whether it was really possible for her to learn new parent coaching skills. Everyone has such doubts at first, and doubts can sabotage your efforts. Joan removed all doubt from her thoughts. She was ruthless in keeping her attention on having a harmonious relationship with her son.

4. New territory: Now you are treading on unfamiliar new territory, and you feel uncertain of yourself. This stage can be intensely exciting or frightening; fear and excitement are merely opposite sides of the coin. Stay motivated by building a "rainbow bridge" between where you are now (problem state) and where you want to be (resource state). The bridge will help you gain the courage to risk making new and unfamiliar choices one step at a time, in alignment with your desired changes. Imagine the golden pot at the end while keeping focused on the step right in front of you.

Joan built her bridge through her desire to be the best parent coach she could be. She really did want her son to become self-determining. Through our work together, she shifted from her need for closeness to honoring his need for some space. Joan cared for her son enough to love him unconditionally from a distance until he felt safe in reconnecting with her, at his own pace.

5. Personal power: You realize that you are the source of your personal power. You are the one you've been waiting for. You are the intervention. You have the power to define who you are and how you want to respond to change, as well as the ability to make new choices, let go of old habits, and develop new ones. No one can do it for you. And even though you may still stumble at times, you know that you have everything needed to support yourself—including the choice to enlist others to help you along this journey.

Joan tapped into her own personal power and allowed herself to feel peaceful about her relationship with her son. It occurred to her that she didn't need to wait until everything between them was perfect; she could experience peace right away, in the present moment.

6. Breakthrough realized: In this final stage, you experience success. You have dissolved the blocks limiting your growth (blocks found in the earlier stages), and now you're soaring as a result of your progress. Be sure to celebrate this event. Many people tend to minimize this stage because change no longer seems like a big deal. It is! Just think back to how you felt at the beginning. Give yourself credit for persistence, and taste the sweetness of victory over your fears.

Eventually, Joan's son learned that he could trust his mother's midcourse correction. She no longer treated him like a child; she was more respectful of his privacy and his need for making his own choices. According to him, "Nothing is more important than hearing my mother say, 'I love you—no matter what.'"

Throughout this program, whether you are reading this book on your own or are learning with your coach or with a group of adults in a workshop setting, you will want to support your development by frequently practicing the exercise below.

Exercise: Access Your Inner Resources

Everyone has had at least one positive experience relating to another person. This exercise will help you deliberately and successfully access this experience and amplify this resourceful state. In doing so, you can then easily transfer your existing skills to future interactions. This short visualization exercise will help you optimize the change process mentioned above, enhancing your success.

1. Sit in a comfortable chair where you won't be interrupted. (Don't do this exercise while driving.) Think of a time in the past when you felt your best relating to another person and were in beautiful rapport. Picture a specific circumstance, environment, and the ease with which you communicated your affection or love for this person. (It doesn't need to be your kid, but it could be.)

2. Notice where you are and what you are doing? Imagine being there now. Step into the experience. Take your time to fully be in this state. See and hear the experience again. Notice your tone of voice and you inner feeling. Make the state as real as possible.

3. Write down what you observed about yourself. What allowed you to relate to this person exquisitely?

   I saw:

   _____

   I heard:

   _____

   I felt:

   _____

4. Clear your mind by taking a few full breaths.

5. Now recall an interaction with your teen that wasn't as smooth as the one above. Select one that you can recall vividly. Step into it. Notice what you see, hear, and feel.

6. Step out of the experience and write down what you observed about yourself this time.

    I saw:

    _____

    I heard:

    _____

    I felt:

    _____

7. What was different between these two experiences? How do you show up when you are relaxed, confident, and in rapport? Record your thoughts here. Please do it now before you forget.

    _____
    _____
    _____
    _____
    _____
    _____
    _____

8. Clear your mind. Take a breath or blink a few times.

9. This time, think of the experience again—the one you want to improve. Take what you have learned about yourself and recreate the experience by inserting your preferred behaviors. See, hear, and feel yourself communicating with and relating to your teen in a positive and harmonious way.

10. How does what you did just now change your experience? Take your time to appreciate this changed state of relating. Enjoy your increased energy and sense of confidence.

    Know that you can recreate this resourceful state at any time in the future. Do this exercise frequently to support yourself in shifting from frustrated parent to parent coach. Then the next time you expect to engage in an interaction, you'll be ready to do so with natural ease and skill.

    What do you want to be sure to remember about placing your resourceful state of mind into other situations? To enhance your retention, write it down.

    _____

    _____

    _____

    _____

    _____

    _____

    _____

Outstanding! This is a very powerful exercise that you can use to improve your relationship with anyone—including your teen, spouse, friend, neighbor or boss. You can use this tool anytime that you're feeling out of your groove. If you experienced some resistance to accessing your inner resources, this simply means that you are more in need of this technique than you consciously realize.

CHAPTER 6

The Power of Positive Why

One of the most important skills to develop as a parent coach is being able to ask well thought out questions. Why questions can either be very powerful in helping us look beneath the surface of things, or they can take us into a trap set by the ego, leaving us feeling depleted. Much depends on what follows after asking "Why?" Suppose I asked you, "Why is it so EASY to have such a wonderful relationship with your teen?" That probably sounds strange or ridiculous. Go ahead and seriously ponder the question anyway.

What is happening in your head? Is your mind short-circuiting? Do you feel some resistance or are you feeling more relaxed? If it feels uncomfortable, that's good. It just means that your brain isn't accustomed to this type of question; it hasn't yet created a neuropathway for it. If you are skeptical, that's understandable. I was, too, at first. It will start to make sense.

Your mind is designed to access information automatically much like a computer finds a file. Without any effort on your part, your mind performs a search within your own database. You may not know it yet, but this little piece of information, will significantly improve the results you're getting in every area of your life, not just in coaching and relating to your teen. You see, IF you earnestly ask yourself a question, your amazing mind cannot choose to ignore it. It must attempt to answer the question you posed.

You already know how to ask questions; you do this regularly, mostly unconsciously. What are some of the questions that you've heard yourself ask? Did they have a positive or negative orientation?

Here are some common examples of questions with a negative spin:

- Why is it so difficult communicating with my teen?
- Why doesn't s/he listen to me?
- Why are we always arguing?
- Why does everything have to turn into high drama?
- Why does s/he refuse to talk with me?

Are some of these questions familiar? Describe the quality of the answers you get when you ask these questions. Are you feeling resourceful? Does it leave you feeling energized or depleted? The feedback I get is that questions with a negative orientation increase frustration levels. Can you see that continuing with these types of questions will only recreate the frustrating experiences from the past?

Questions that focus on the negative cannot prompt your mind to locate productive answers, inner resources, or creative solutions. Look at it this way. Say, you are doing a key word search on your computer. You, not your computer, determine what words to enter. The computer will automatically conduct a search based on the words you gave it. If your words are focused on what you don't want, all you get is more data supporting just that. It's as if your computer-mind reaches into your storehouse of old beliefs and confirms what you believed to be true about yourself in the past. Thus, it only serves to ensure that you will recreate your past. It does not support you in changing it for the better. Will your computer access data that does not match your key word selection merely because you wish your situation were different? Of course not! Questions with a negative orientation will quickly sabotage your good intentions.

Please understand that this method has nothing to do with being optimistic or pessimistic. It's not about whether the glass is half empty or half full. We are NOT focusing on the glass; we are focusing on content, the water! When you put water in the glass, you have water. If you put orange juice in the glass, you have orange juice. It's that simple. What key words are you putting in your computer-mind?

Let's see what happens when you change the structure of your question to include a presupposition, words that describe already having what you really want. Again, if you sincerely ask this question, your mind HAS to search for this information. Are you warming up to this idea by now? Realize that you are retraining your brain. Just repeat your question. Human beings learn through repetition. No one becomes a black-diamond skier following their first attempt at skiing!

Remember, your mind is already searching for answers. So, let's have you ask a question based on what you really want to experience. And because most of us love to ask "why" questions, we'll have you do just that. What I want for you is to begin living your preferred vision right now. So, suppose your future is here now; ask yourself, "Why is it so easy for me to relate to my teen?" Your mind will automatically search for files matching the key words "easy relating with my teen" and present you with matching data. Notice what thoughts show up for you. How do you feel? Did your mind attempt to find answers? Most people feel more relaxed, lighter, or encouraged. One client mentioned that the mere paradox of the question caused him to smile and lighten up.

Sometimes, there's a delay before corresponding files show up. That's okay. It's NOT necessary to have your mind immediately present you with all the answers you are seeking. Your mind will continue to seek answers while you're busy doing something else—while you're taking a shower, sleeping, gardening, or whatever. The answers will continue to show up in your life. You are simply responsible for selecting key words that match your desired outcome.

Let me illustrate how this method works even when you are initially skeptical. My client Sally, a management consultant, complained that her 18-year-old high maintenance teen, Sarah, flies off the handle easily and expects Sally to handle situations that her teen could easily take care of. Sally wanted to set better boundaries for herself and thereby teach her teen to begin taking more self responsibility, but she didn't know how. She'd feel guilty when she didn't immediately take over to help her daughter. We discussed using my parent coach-approach to help redirect her teen (you'll learn more about this later). Sally was very concerned and believed it would be too difficult to coach Sarah based on their past conversations. I suggested Sally ask herself, "Why is it so EASY to coach Sarah?"

At first, Sally laughed and didn't think I was serious. In fact, since her mind habitually thought about why it was so DIFFICULT to get Sarah to do things for herself, her mind was stuck on this well-traveled track, and her usual "negative stuff" bubbled up first. Her mind didn't take the question seriously. I asked Sally to ask the question again as sincerely as she could. This time, her computer-mind registered blank, "file not found." Excellent! Now her mind could keep working on finding answers. Still feeling stumped, Sally was skeptical, but she committed to keep asking herself why it was easy to coach Sarah whenever Sarah popped into her mind. The very next day, this is what I heard from Sally:

"I just got off the phone from my daughter, who called all upset and having computer troubles. I asked her 'who could you contact to help you with

this?' She said she didn't know, but I kept at it. 'Do you have the number of Microsoft? Do you have the number to Compaq support?' Soon, she was looking them up. I wrapped the call with 'is this the best time for you to make this call?' (She was really negative and upset.) She said, 'No, I need to calm down first.' The end. So, thanks!!! It worked!"

Practice posting a positive question—one that has what you want to experience imbedded in the question. The magic is in the quality of the search, the key words that you command your mind to work on. Said differently, the emphasis needs to be on what your mind will be focusing on. Focus on the content, not the glass. If you focus on juice when you really want champagne, the result will be disappointing because there is no match. Keep your focus on what you want, not on what you don't want.

Phrasing your question in the positive vs. negative will direct your mind to finding useful information because the focus is on believing you have access to the answer. You will soon experience first-hand the truth about the way empowering questions will impact the quality of your life. Anytime you feed your mind questions that are in alignment with your goal of knowing the answer—the solution—you will succeed. This is also true for situations or problems that don't seem to have answers yet.

Exercise

A Let's practice with the following questions, all phrased with a negative orientation, focusing on what you don't want to experience. Rewrite them into questions that focus on what you prefer to experience. Be sure to use the sentence stem "Why is it so EASY to ...?" I'll get you started.

1. Why do I allow myself to get frustrated?
    Rewrite: Why is it so EASY for me to stay relaxed?

_____

2. Why is it hard to retrain my brain?

    Rewrite: Why is it so EASY _____?

    _____

3. Why isn't it possible for me to learn this method quickly?

    Rewrite: Why is it so EASY _____?

    _____

Good work!

B   Now practice the power of positive why using your own recurring top why questions (that are posed in a negative orientation). Afterwards, rephrase them so that your active mind can get to work productively.

1. _____

Rewrite: _____?

2. _____

Rewrite: _____?

3. _____

Rewrite: _____?

Remember just keep repeating your powerful questions without HAVING to have any answers just yet. If answers appear, that's great. Keep using the sentence stem, "Why is it so EASY…," and the answers will come.

In summary, the reason that the Power of Positive Why is so important for you to do now, before you do anything else, is because it: (1) interrupts your old pattern of thinking; (2) lifts you up; when you have hope, you tap into a renewed energy source to take the next steps that lead to what you want to experience; (3) creates a new neuropathway for the brain, allowing change to take place. The above steps are necessary for preparing a new space for developing a new positive orientation.

Imagine what would happen if you planted new seeds over old plants with an established root system. Any gardener knows that the old plants would over flourish, preventing the new seeds from growing. In our case, a new pattern of thinking (young seeds) don't have a chance to push through the extensive root system (old neuropathways) until you create space with a blade (the power of why). Afterwards, through repetition and some linear time the new roots will develop (new neuropathway) and take hold.

Congratulations, you have just learned that by changing the quality of the questions you ask yourself, you change your results! (If you didn't do the above exercises, go back and do them now. Nothing in your life will change if you don't). Many clients utilize their increased energy and start to act on their answers right away.

Some of my clients get so excited about using this technique they can't wait to share it with their teens. Just imagine if you had learned to use this tool while you were a teenager. How much easier would your life have been?

PART TWO

Clearing the Path

CHAPTER 7

Parenting Styles

In order to heal, build or enhance your relationship with your teen, it's vital to first have a clear understanding of your current reality. There are many factors, conscious and unconscious, that influence your parenting style and therefore your level of effectiveness. It's difficult to coach your teen to success when you lack awareness about your own parenting style and have not yet fully resolved your own disappointments concerning the parenting you experienced.

Imagine that each of us, from birth, is equipped with a built in camcorder that begins filming without interruption the moment you take your first breath. Everything you see, hear, feel, and experience is permanently recorded. Countless reels, all beautifully catalogued are stored in your unconscious mind. Much of it is repetitive—both the helpful scenes and the harmful ones. So, only a small portion of the content is beneficial. Unlike a camcorder that you operate consciously, no editing takes place. Your computer mind accesses this information on demand whether you are fully aware of it or not, based on your predominant emotional and mental patterns.

What does all this have to do with parenting you ask? It has everything to do with it because we are all strongly influenced by our inner recordings. Whether you are a parent who walks behind your teen pushing and criticizing or one that walks in front pulling and cajoling, you have been influenced by the sum total of your recorded experience. Without becoming more conscious of your past influences, you are bound to repeat old patterns, particularly under stress. More than ever before, today's teens need parents who will walk alongside and partner with teens, respectfully offering them choices and resources.

We have spent the first 18 years of our lives adapting to our childhood, often learning outdated habits that are self-limiting or perhaps even destructive to having healthy relationships. As an adult, have you noticed that you are beginning to become more like your mother or father? Where in your life are you experiencing problems or pain? How are your habitual responses to your teens (or to life) serving you? When we automatically repeat our childhood strategies as adults without updating them, we stay mired in the past. In bringing childhood beliefs—when our mental acuity wasn't fully developed yet—into the present causes us to miss golden opportunities to evolve. When we become free from our history by acknowledging our past, we can easily embrace new ways of thinking and being. Only then can we indeed be the best parents we intend to be.

CHAPTER 8

Parenting Styles Self-Assessment

This self-assessment provides important insights into your current parenting style. In each situation described below, quickly (without thinking about it too much) circle the answer that reflects your predominant response. If nothing seems to fit, select the answer that most closely resembles how you would respond to the situations presented.

1. Your 16-year-old daughter loves make-up and has recently been wearing lots of glitter around her eyes.

   (a) You roll your eyes when you see her and say nothing.

   (b) You notice it and say lightly, "I see that you're really into glitter right now. How does it make you feel when you wear it?"

(c) You think it looks cheap and tell her she had better wash it off before she leaves the house with you.

2. Your 14-year-old son is very bright and creative, but gets bored at school and sees no value in doing his homework. You see him watching TV and suspect he's once again avoiding doing his homework.

   (a) You are frustrated with him and tell him he had better get his homework done or else he'll be punished.

   (b) You don't bring up the subject because you don't want to risk getting into an argument.

   (c) You schedule a time to talk with him later in the evening and ask him to share his feelings about school, homework. You listen deeply and discuss what the payoff is for doing the work and for not doing the work.

3. Your 18-year-old daughter promised to help you clean out the attic Saturday afternoon. She was to have arrived over an hour ago. She hasn't contacted you even though you already left her a message on her cell phone. You start without her. When she finally arrives, you

   (a) Say nothing; you're glad she's here now to help you with your project.

   (b) Ask what happened and find out she got distracted and was lax about her commitment. You enforce your predetermined consequences.

   (c) Angrily let her know that being stood up is not acceptable and berate her for being irresponsible.

4. You've raised your 15-year-old son in the Christian tradition. Today he announces that Christianity doesn't make sense to him and he wants to explore becoming a Buddhist.

   (a) You're shocked and hurt that your son is rejecting your religion and related concepts you hold so dear. You get defensive and believe the only reason he is saying this is to upset you.

(b) You tell yourself it's not important and dismiss it.

(c) You are disappointed and don't take it personally. You realize that your teen needs to make his own decisions about spirituality.

5. Your 14-year-old daughter is bringing her first boyfriend to the house. You've met him before briefly and you feel uneasy.

(a) You are pleasant and attempt to get to know the boy better, engaging him in conversation.

(b) You make sure you are home and you're polite; you keep your misgivings to yourself and begin plotting how you can keep him away from your daughter.

(c) You busy yourself with another task upon the boy's arrival.

6. You have a conversation with your 17-year-old son about going to college. You believe in higher education and want him to obtain an undergraduate degree. He thinks it's a waste of time and dreams of starting his own business.

(a) You tell him he's going to college first, and then if he still wants to go into business, he can do it armed with a college degree.

(b) You realize that there are many people who have been wildly successful without a college degree and let go of your dream for him.

(c) You ask him to tell you more about his plans for his dream; afterwards, together you create an action plan that clearly outlines the next several steps to help your son attain his goal.

7. You gave your 18-year-old daughter a beautiful Waterford crystal bowl worth $400 for her birthday. You hoped she would enjoy it for many years to come. Shortly thereafter, you discovered that your daughter gave this exquisite bowl to her best friend as a wedding present.

(a) You keep your disappointment to yourself and decide to give her presents that are less expensive (or meaningful) from now on.

(b) You can hardly see straight, pick up the phone and cry, "How could you do that?"

(c) You understand that the bowl is now her property and honor her decision while respectfully (and honestly) sharing your true feelings.

8. Your teenage son is developing interests that are very different from your own. You don't understand teenage-ese, can't stand the new music, and dislike the teen-culture dress code.

(a) You want to stay connected to your son, so you stay flexible, learn more about his choices, and refrain from criticizing.

(b) You tell your son you don't approve of his taste and try to convince him that he needs to change.

(c) You neither support nor disapprove; you're ambivalent.

9. Your 17-year-old daughter informs you that she got a speeding ticket.

(a) You don't think much of it. (Maybe you even pay the fine for her.)

(b) You ask her what she plans on doing differently next time.

(c) You're furious and suspend her driving privileges for one week.

10. Your 16-year-old daughter wants to get her tongue pierced along with her classmates.

(a) You are totally against it and forbid her to get it done.

(b) You can't imagine anyone wanting to do that, and you encourage her to do research on the pros and cons so that she can make an informed decision.

(c) You would prefer that she didn't do it and leave it at that.

11. Your 19-year-old daughter complains that you are much more committed to and generous with her younger sister, after she found out you funded most of her class trip.

(a) You dismiss it and tell her, "Life's not fair; get used to it."

(b) You admit that it might appear that way due to the amount given to her sister this time, and ask her to recall the times you paid for volleyball camp.

(c) You tell her you'll think about what she said, hoping that she'll forget about it.

12. Your 13-year-old son felt rejected by one of his best friends today and is having an emotional meltdown.

(a) You ignore him and hope he'll work it out for himself soon.

(b) You give him some space to calm down and then schedule a time to give him the opportunity to talk about it with you.

(c) You tell him, "Stop blowing everything out of proportion. Grow up. I don't want you moping around me."

13. Your 13-year-old daughter feels discouraged and tells you she can't do anything right.

(a) You say, "That's not true. You're exaggerating."

(b) You respond, "I can feel your frustration; it's not fun to feel that way. What's causing you to feel bad right now?"

(c) You reply, "Don't worry about it. You're a very bright kid."

14. Your 14-year-old nephew has joined your family for a vacation. He doesn't know how to swim. His fear of water is keeping him from enjoying his summer at the lake house with his cousins.

(a) You encourage him to join in with the others and expect that the peer pressure will cause him to conquer his fear.

(b) You say, "Don't be a sissy. How would you like for me to push you in? That's how I learned to swim."

(c) You say, "Lot's of people are afraid of water. Tell me more about what you are specifically concerned about? Maybe together we can find a way to help you enjoy the water."

15. Your 19-year-old son is at college. You want him to get a business degree and take over the family commercial real estate business. He'd rather join the Peace Corps.

(a) You let him do just as he wants.

(b) You threaten to cut him off financially in order to get your way.

(c) You take an interest in the Peace Corps and help him achieve his goal.

16. You asked your 14-year-old daughter to set the table for the family dinner tonight. She said okay, but it's been 15 minutes and she still hasn't started.
    (a) You yell at her, "Why don't you do as you're told? I want you to set the table NOW!"
    (b) You sigh and decide it's easier to set the table yourself.
    (c) You say, "How about setting the table now? This way, we can enjoy being at the dinner table together, instead of having a battle over cooperation."

17. Your teenage son has difficulty staying tuned in when others speak. He interrupts or gets distracted.
    (a) You offer the following, "I've noticed that you seem to have difficulty waiting until someone is done talking and staying on track. I can help with that. Would you like me to give you some tips?"
    (b) You say, "Stop interrupting. It's rude!"
    (c) You tolerate it because you think he might have some ADD tendencies.

18. You saw your teenage daughter scratch the passenger door of the family car as she quickly backed out of the garage on her way to meet a friend.
    (a) You run out of the house and in a loud voice, ask "Why did you do that?"
    (b) You shake your head and take care of the scratch later.
    (c) You talk to her that evening and together work out a plan for her to get the car door fixed and paid for.

Now score yourself using the key found in Appendix 3.

What your parenting style score means:

43-54 You are a **participative parent coach**

You believe that everyone deserves respect. You establish reasonable rules and guidelines with input from your teen. You provide solid guidance by staying connected to your heart and your head. You are open, flexible, and listen closely. You're good at clarifying issues and giving reasons for your decisions and requests. Your focus is on how to promote self-responsibility and you model effective life skills. Teens are given plenty of latitude to practice making their own choices. Appropriate consequences or problem-solving consistently follow misbehavior. Emphasis is placed on learning, not punishment. Teens raised in this style quickly learn to be responsible, embrace change, and make wise choices. This parenting style is ideal for today's environment of rapid-fire change and a business climate where creative and collaborative problem-solving are prized.

Typical quotes:

"What are your options?"

"Be true to yourself."

"What do you think will happen if you do that?"

24-42 You are a **permissive parent**

You take a hands-off approach to parenting and believe that teens learn best by encouraging them to experiment on their own. You are more comfortable being a buddy than a parent. You have few limits, value being unconventional, and provide little information about expected behavior. You often ignore misbehavior and rarely intervene, leaving your teen to find his or her way, without much support. You believe that life is the teacher. You detach prematurely and often the teen interprets this as a lack of love. Teens raised in this style are often more creative and nonconforming. Without providing a range of life skills and focused guidance to self-discovery, these teens feel insecure, make poor choices, and learn the hard way. They can more easily fall into the victim mentality trap. It takes much longer for teens to become productive adults. This parenting style doesn't adequately prepare teens for our fast-paced society.

Typical quotes:

"Just don't get into any trouble."

"Ask your Mother (Father)."

"You'll figure it out."

18-23 You are an **authoritarian parent**

You prefer a hands-on (controlling) approach to parenting. You have strong feelings about what is right and wrong. You tell teens what to do and what not to do. You have a long list of rules that you have unilaterally created and are not negotiable. Punishment is strictly enforced. You expect your teens to take on your beliefs and values without question. You believe that since you are responsible for your teens, you have the right to make decisions for them. Emphasis is on obedience. Teens raised in this style have difficulty being flexible, take an all-or-nothing approach, are fearful of change, and become defensive and defiant. In a dynamic society that values choice and innovation, this style is outdated; it might have been adequate in the past when we lived in a world with little change, but it does not prepare our young people for success today.

Typical quotes:

"I'm the parent, you're the child."

"I'll give you something to cry about."

"Do it because I said so."

Although you might be drawing from several parenting styles, depending on the situation, most parents have a distinct preference for one of the styles described above. These three styles represent an evolution in parenting. The authoritarian style was prevalent up until the '50s. Then beginning in the '60s, in rebellion to rigid rules and strict punishment, the pendulum swung to the opposite extreme where the permissive parenting style became popular. Later, as we moved into the '80s, our society experienced a rate of change never before thought possible. We now value choice, creativity, collaboration, and innovation. In response to our rapidly changing society, the participative parent coach-approach was born.

My question to you is, "Are you still driving a Studebaker?" No doubt you have changed vehicles several times by now and you are fully upgraded. You've probably also upgraded your home, your furniture, and your electronic "toys." But when was the last time you upgraded your parenting skills? Why stay stuck in the past? Now is your opportunity to learn new skills, to upgrade from parent to parent coach.

"Fifty years from now, it will not matter
what kind of car you drove,
what kind of house you lived in,
how much you had in your bank account,
or what your clothes looked like.
But the world may be a little better because
You were important in the life of a child."

Anonymous

CHAPTER 9

Top 10 Qualities of Successful Parent-Teen Relationships

Have you ever wondered why some family relationships are strong, close, and successful while others struggle? No matter what type of relationship you are in, all relationships require focused attention and deep caring. The following list will aid you in remembering to nurture and strengthen your relationships by inviting your mind to meet your heart.

1. Heart
    When you are a parent with heart, you'll demonstrate affection, kindness, compassion, and daily expressions of love in both words and deeds.

2. Empathy

   When you are willing to temporarily "live" in the world of another to identify feelings, thoughts, and beliefs, your personal bond strengthens.

3. Adaptability

   When you choose to be flexible with your expectations during new or challenging circumstances, you will weather the storm with your relationships intact.

4. Respect

   When you treat teens (and all family members) with high regard simply because they have inherent value as human beings, you enhance self-esteem.

5. Trust

   When you are trustworthy–predictably dependable–and you create a safe environment, your teens will be more confident, ethical, and better adjusted.

6. Appreciation

   When you look for the positive, praise, and express gratitude, you will be fulfilling one of your teen's most basic human needs.

7. Commitment

   When you are dedicated to the well-being of your relationships, you will be loyal and motivated to devote quality time to each family member, resulting in enjoying a firm family foundation.

8. Conflict resolution

   When you view disagreements, stress, or crisis as opportunities for learning about each other, you will promote growth for all involved.

9. Enhanced communication

   When you use the 7-step parent coaching approach, you will

naturally create enhanced communication where each person freely expresses their feelings and thoughts, is fully heard, and given the utmost consideration.

10. **Support**
When there is a clear understanding of responsibilities and teens have a voice in decision making and consequences, you will be successfully supporting your teen's passage from child to adult.

Together these initial letters spell HeartAcces(s). Keep this acronym in mind as you continue to read, learn, and practice the 7-step approach to *Coaching Your Teen to Success.*

"Being a parent is not a natural ability all of us are born with. It is a learning process that takes time, patience, and the development of skills."

Charles Schaefer, Ph.D.

CHAPTER 10

The Three Parenting Pitfalls

To consistently experience having the above top ten qualities in your relationship with your teen, you must first be willing to be honest with yourself. If you are feeling tired, angry or stuck, chances are you are hiding your true feelings. People lie to themselves when they have trouble accepting their feelings or the truth about a situation. If you don't allow yourself to get in touch with what you are really thinking, you will be subject to parenting pitfalls and not be fully available to absorb the transformational techniques offered in this book. You also run the risk of passing these pitfalls along to your children.

As humans, our primary emotional need is love, the desire for connection. The three pitfalls that block you from connecting to love and that keep you from having a successful relationship with your teen are: anger, fear, and guilt. Keep in mind that when the word love is used, it's not just a feeling; it's also behavior (being kind) and taking action (expressing love). Let's begin with anger. When you understand the purpose of anger, you can more easily channel the energy of anger—yours and your teens—productively so that you can both experience more harmony (love).

ANGER

Anger is an emotional response with a purpose. Its positive purpose is to notify you that change needs to occur in order to return to love. It signals that you have lost your effectiveness on behalf of yourself or someone else to produce necessary change. For instance, you might be angry because you lost your job. Your anger can now motivate you to locate a position or career that is much more in alignment with your strengths. Anger is useful because it serves as your automatic biofeedback that love is in short supply and prompts action. It lets you know that either you are not being loving enough with yourself (tolerating a job that is unbearable) or others are not treating you with love (working for an abusive boss). In an ideal world, everyone would be enlightened and we wouldn't need anger to flag that something needs our attention.

Is it difficult for you to accept that anger is an important feeling to be fully acknowledged? Then you might be associating anger with rage. Rage stems from an utter feeling of powerlessness and deep sadness; it is uncontrolled, abusive, and destructive. If you find yourself overreacting, you are drawing from a reservoir of suppressed and accumulated anger that can easily turn into rage. In the initial stages of anger, some love is still present, not so with rage. Or, perhaps you were raised with the belief that it isn't nice to be angry and you stuffed your anger to appear good or spiritual. Either way, you probably didn't learn that a dose of anger can be used for good. The consequence of unresolved anger is sabotaged intentions. Trust between yourself and your teen is negatively impacted when you vacillate between being loving and supportive one moment and attacking and critical the next. By holding your anger inside, you are much more likely to eventually explode and become abusive, exhibiting the behavior you wanted to avoid.

Most people have no idea that unexpressed anger is deceptively insidious. Why? Because anger is an intense emotion and if it's not properly channeled or released, it will be stored in the body and contribute to anger patterns in your household. Parents that pride themselves on denying their anger can expect it to surface full force through another family member. These clueless parents nearly always wonder, "Where did all that anger come from?" Without acknowledging and clearing anger regularly, your anger will trigger others and vice versa. Face it, anger begets more anger. All of us generally recognize anger in someone else, especially in teens, before getting in touch with our own. I often hear, "I didn't even know I was angry."

Realize that anger is a catalyst for change, a course correction. The instrument panel on an aircraft flashes an amber warning light for pilots that a change needs to occur. If the condition persists and still no action is taken, a red danger light and signal follow. It might help to think of the amber light as the onset of anger and the red light as rage, notifying you that something either within you, or outside of you, needs to change. If you ignore these signals, you can expect destruction.

Being honest and reporting the onset of anger is the first step in producing positive change. You can do this by saying, "I acknowledge that I am angry about _____." Ask yourself, "What can I learn from my anger?" "What is it prompting me to say or do differently?" "What requests do I need to make of others?" Parents and teens that use an assertive or collaborative approach to handling disagreements and anger, stay solution-focused. Of course, respectfully expressing your true feelings does not guarantee that all of your requests will be granted and your needs automatically met. It does ensure that you will not be accumulating more anger that, if unexpressed, can result in rage. While unexpressed anger shows up as withdrawal, defensiveness or wanting to prematurely end the argument, the opposite extreme is characterized by throwing objects, shouting, swearing or worse. Both are distancing strategies that lead to retreat instead of resolving the conflict.

Behind anger is the need for more love. When you are honest about your feelings, you feel better (expand love) because you will have upheld your integrity. The powerful love you feel for yourself as a result of empowering yourself, when you have the courage to respectfully express anger (not dump), is very healing. Then it becomes possible for you to sprinkle expressions of caring and warmth in the midst of your argument, keeping the communication lines open. In this way, you are able to talk constructively. In addition, your kids will learn from you how to be in emotional integrity and be equipped with healthy patterns when it's their turn to be parents. Acknowledging anger and thereby increasing the supply of love frees you from the past and produces profound change.

Paul, a father of two preteens, realized that he was still angry with his dad about what happened to Paul's car when he was a teenager. Dad convinced Paul not to take his car with him when he left for college. Then, when Paul returned home during the holidays he was shocked to discover that his dad had sold his car! The only explanation he got was that the car took up too much space and got in the way. Paul was angry but wasn't truthful about his feelings due to the conditioning he received from his parents. "My impression was that if you loved someone, you didn't disagree with them." His parents prided themselves on never having any disagreements. And being disagreeable (angry and arguing) was not tolerated in this family. Paul learned early on to stuff his anger.

Paul carried the parenting patterns he grew up with into his own family. One day Paul came home from the office and found that his 11-year-old daughter, Karen, had had an argument with a neighbor girl. Paul took a dislike to this girl and without discussing it with his wife (a stay-at-home mom), he informed Karen, "From now on, you are not to play with this girl." Karen was furious about this edict and secretly complained to her mother. Her mom didn't agree with her husband, said nothing to him, but didn't enforce the new rule. Paul had no idea that he had repeated his parents' unhealthy "no disagreements allowed" pattern—behavior that when he was on the receiving end caused him much pain and confusion. Without an intervention, Paul's children will likely perpetuate the problem. You can see from this example that when anger is dismissed and stored, the opportunity for positive change is lost.

Acknowledging and then releasing the anger provides opportunities to experience preferred changes. As one parent said, "Simply having the awareness has made a difference with my son." In contrast, angry outbursts, including rage, occur when anger is allowed to accumulate within. When feelings are chronically shut down, they cease healthy functioning. But make no mistake, the emotions don't disappear, they are merely stored and often erupt in frightening ways. They show up inwardly as disease or outwardly as uncontrolled explosions that can take the shape of a 13-year-old boy threatening his mother at home with a kitchen knife or an 18-year-old girl lashing out by physically attacking her sister in a public place. In both of these instances, these children were feeling powerless and temporarily lacked any connection to love. It doesn't have to be this way. Start with yourself, stop denying or hiding your anger. The best way to reverse rage is to begin before it becomes a problem.

The positive purpose of anger is not efficiently realized when anger is prolonged. For every hour that you remain angry and internalize it, it takes your body from 8-12 hours to recover and return to equilibrium. That's assuming you don't get angry again in the meantime! Not only is this unproductive time (time that could be used to create positive change), it also creates an overabundance of free radicals that can cause damage to your cells and tissues, contributing to the development of various degenerative conditions.

Whether you believe that you have suppressed anger or not, please do not skip over the important exercises below, especially if you are someone who is uncomfortable with expressing your feelings.

Exercise: Acknowledge Your Anger

NOTE: The exercises in this section are not intended as a substitute for professional help from mental health professionals.

A. When was the last time you expressed anger? Write down when and where below.

_____

_____

_____

_____

B. What change did your anger help bring about? How?

_____

_____

_____

_____

If not, why not?

_____

_____

_____

_____

Typical answers are: "I didn't express my anger." "I waited too long and missed my opportunity." "My anger had built up and I expressed my anger too forcefully."

_____

_____

How will you take advantage of the opportunity anger brings next time?

_____

_____

_____

_____

C. Think back to your childhood or adolescence. What frustrated (or angered) you about the parenting you received? Use the sentence stem, "I acknowledge that I feel angry about _____" and record your feelings and thoughts below.

MOM

_____

_____

_____

_____

DAD

_____

_____

_____

_____

OTHER ADULT

_____

_____

_____

_____

Know that a thought is not a feeling. (For information about how to distinguish between a thought and a feeling, refer to my previous book, *Less Drama, More Fun*. You can go to **www.enhancedlife.com** or www.amazon.com.) If you are having trouble feeling, take a pen or pencil and focus on an unresolved hurtful event. Draw whatever shows up without thinking about it first. Just start putting your pen to paper. It doesn't have to look like anything in particular. It can be squiggly lines, shapes or figures. Just trust that you cannot do it wrong. (This usually takes a minute or two. If it takes longer, you're trying too hard. In that case, imagine yourself as a child drawing with your favorite crayon.) Use the space below.

1. Look at your drawing. Give it a caption.

2. Record your insights.

D. How have these experiences and frustrations impacted your relationship with your teen?

_____

_____

_____

_____

E. As a result of your new awareness, what would you like to be doing differently?

_____

_____

_____

_____

FEAR

Whether you are afraid of your anger, of losing control, loss of love or of not having enough love in your relationships, this section on fear has been included especially for you. The purpose of fear is to alert us that life-threatening danger is ahead. It instantly activates the ingrained "fight or flight" response and serves as immediate protection before the mind can sort through survival strategies. Like anger, fear was not intended to be long-lasting. When fear is prolonged, it's too hard on the body; it depletes physical, mental, and emotional resources. Such anxiety defeats the purpose of fear with regard to real immediate danger. It's like the boy crying wolf.

Everyone experiences fear from time to time. Yet few admit it. Fear is often denied and unexpressed. To dissolve fear, you must first be honest with yourself that you have fear. Once you acknowledge it, you can act on it.

Be aware that fear is often hidden behind anger. For example Eric's father, Tom, had been educated in Europe and began a family late in life. Tom was "old school": distant, critical, very strict, and not at all demonstrative. When Eric was 16 years old, he managed to live with another family to finish school while Tom remarried and moved to another city with Eric's siblings. Eric had accumulated much anger as a result of not having felt enough love from his father and had difficulty with authority figures (i.e., teachers), especially those who were confrontational. Eric conceded that in his father's own way, there was love, but he wasn't able to experience it. Eric hadn't realized that beneath his anger, lay the fear of "not being good enough." Going further, he discovered that the core fear was a "loss of love." I call both of these fears "pseudo fears" because unlike the fear of a "loss of life," they don't protect us. Pseudo fears just create filters where fear becomes a default position. Here feedback is heard as criticism or attack. Once Eric realized that the root of his suffering was due to his pseudo fear, he was able to take responsibility for his tendency to take things personal (assumptions that others deliberately sought to wound him) and make better choices, instead of responding defensively.

In understanding the positive purpose of your feelings, you can be more appreciative of all of them. Consider adopting the notion that each feeling provides you with a message and an opportunity for growth. Picture the range of feelings on a color spectrum. What if you don't like the color orange? Could you get rid of orange? No, of course not! So, let's say you don't like the feeling of fear. In the same way that you cannot eliminate orange from the color chart, you cannot eradicate fear from your range of emotions. However, you can accept that fear exists just as the color orange exists. You don't have to wear an orange jacket! Just so with awareness, you can choose whether to wear the mantle of fear or not.

Fearful thinking feeds fear. It's contagious and limiting. Once you are trapped in the quicksand of fear, it can take enormous energy to get free of it. When you acknowledge fear and use it constructively, it can serve as a motivator. For instance, the fear of "not being good enough" can also be used to reach further and accomplish more. If unattended, however, fear can expand exponentially and could very well put you at risk. That's when your mind runs amok with an assortment of frightening and far-fetched scenarios. Think about it, have you noticed how clouded your thinking is when you are fearful (or angry)?

Let's look at this situation with Selena, a much older sister to her brother, a freshman in college. Selena took on the controlling parental role her mother modeled, during his preteen years when their mother became very ill. Ever since her brother declared his independence from her when he left for college, Selena felt hurt and rejected. He no longer talks to her regularly and keeps his personal life private. Selena's fear of losing her influence and control over her brother became overpowering. She desperately wanted to force him to continue checking in with her about his every move. Naturally, he resisted. Lacking information, Selena's mind ran wild with worry. Without being willing to own her fear, blaming her brother for her pain, she wasn't able to give fear a reality-check.

Through our work together, Selena began taking responsibility for herself and realized that she wasn't getting positive results because she was struggling too much due to her unresolved fear. Once she was able to acknowledge her own anxieties and insecurities, she let go of her struggle. She learned that problems are exacerbated by continually rehashing them. In having the courage to face her fears, she felt empowered. It gave her the strength to shift from feeling sorry for herself to being open to upgrading and redefining her relationship with her younger brother. Lauren is the mother of two adult children (early 20s), but emotionally they are much younger. According to Lauren, her mother was the consummate caretaker.

Lauren felt stifled during her teenage years and admitted, "At sixteen, I escaped when my mother suddenly died." Initially, Lauren was blind to recognizing how she was perpetuating the caretaker pattern with her own children. Lauren continued to manage their lives for them even though they have both graduated from college, because she's convinced that they'll botch it up if she doesn't.

Once Lauren understood that her interference doesn't prepare them for the future, but actually assures their dependence on her, a weight was lifted. She knew she no longer wanted to "be her mother," but now a new fear surfaced. What if her adult children decide to withhold love from her because she's abruptly changing her role? Once again, in the context of relationships, a common fear is "loss of love." After our rehearsal, Lauren was surprised at how easy it was for her to have honest and supportive conversations with her son and daughter without feeling fearful or guilty.

Exercise: Five Steps to Managing Fear

A. Now it's your turn. What are you afraid of when it comes to interacting with your kids? What do you intuitively know that you need to start doing or stop doing that you're anxious about? What are you afraid to know about your teen? Write your fears here:

_____

_____

_____

_____

An important reason to be honest about your fear relates to emotional integrity. When you deny fear (or any feeling) you are out of integrity with yourself. As you learn to fully accept and love yourself, this will become easier for you. Know that love for yourself—and others—is compromised when you keep the truth from yourself.

B. Take each identified fear and apply this five-step formula for each one:

1. Feel the fear fully without suppressing it. Where in your body do you feel it most? (Identify body parts.)

2. Acknowledge the fear and accept it as part of the range of human emotions. Accept your humanness by saying, "It's okay for me to feel the fear."

3. Observe the fear without consciously analyzing it. Just note any images that arise naturally, then let them go.

4. Embrace your fear without judging it (i.e., without making it wrong for being there.)

5. Relax by taking in more oxygen. Consciously inhale and exhale while focusing your breath on your fear. Direct it to the body parts you identified in step 1. Do this breath work until you feel that a shift has taken place (usually from five to 30 minutes, depending on the degree of the fear). Record your insights here.

_____

_____

_____

_____

Clients report that self-confidence and self-love expand after using this five-step method. Check in with yourself at least once a day and ask, "What am I feeling?" If what you are feeling is causing you to be tired or irritated, use the above tool to get centered. Remember fear, worry, and negativity shut out your connection to love and ultimately to having fulfilling parent-teen relationships.

GUILT

Guilt stems from both anger and fear unexpressed. When you feel guilty it means that you have unresolved anger from the past coupled with the fear of honestly expressing your anger in the present. Yes, really! Keep reading and it will make more sense. The reason you feel so miserable when you feel guilty is because its positive purpose is to get you to tell the truth in order to feel whole again. Harboring guilt is counterproductive.

The longer you keep the guilt, the worse it feels. Some people, disconnected from loving themselves, feel that they deserve to feel guilty and get stuck there. Others realize that they need to do something to liberate themselves from guilt, but they seek to do this outside of themselves. One common example is when the parents have demanding careers and they feel guilty about not spending sufficient time with their children. They give their kids plenty of money or expensive gifts, hoping to alleviate their own guilt. Throwing money at the problem is a temporary fix, a Band-Aid. Not only does this approach keep you from permanently lifting your guilt, it doesn't meet your teen's need on an emotional level, nor does it prepare your teen for the reality of adult living.

Parents who divorce are prone to work off their guilt in ways that are not healthy. Take Disney Dad for example. This father lives out of state and whenever his son visits (a few weeks during the summer) he lavishes him with gifts and treats their time together as if they're on vacation. During his stay, Disney Dad abdicates his parenting role and treats him like a buddy. Money is laid down freely, but he rarely talks to his son during the rest of the year, leaving a lonely teenager. But the guilt by the uninvolved father remains.

In this case study both parents lived under the same roof. Don, a traveling sales representative with two teens, is married to Joyce, an accident-prone woman who often injured herself. He dreaded leaving his daughters with their mother because she had difficulty keeping herself safe, let alone her children. He was home about three days a week and when at the house he took care of much of the household duties, including the cooking. Don felt guilty about his job-related absences from home, so he brought nice gifts, but didn't ask the girls or anyone else to help out. As a result of his choice to silently shoulder everything himself, his daughters developed a "what have you done for me lately" attitude. Don also felt guilty about not giving his career the attention it deserved.

Both girls are in college now, but they mirror back the guilt he still carries inside. They're rarely satisfied and continue to trigger his guilt by pointing out that he's not available to them whenever they call. He's even reluctant to terminate telephone conversations with them and arrives late to meetings, because he wants to avoid any potential fall-out with them.

Don had a history of being disconnected from this anger. He is just beginning to realize that by not having acknowledged the anger early on—with regard to feeling burdened (taking on his wife's responsibilities in addition to his own)—his suppressed anger developed into a condition. Since Don failed to utilize the energy of anger to create change (anger's purpose) at the onset when it was still safe, his anger continued to accumulate. When anger is allowed to build, it is even more difficult not to fear the potential ramifications of expressing it. His suppressed anger and fear continued to produce guilt no matter how many sacrifices he made for the girls!

At this point, Don's hidden anger has lost its power to create the change that was necessary when the anger first surfaced. Had he acknowledged his anger, Don could have found a solution where his needs and his family's needs were honored. However, Don found out that it is not too late to be honest about his true feelings, to acknowledge the anger and the fear underneath the guilt. Being honest about anger and fear will cause a return to emotional integrity and this in turn will release the guilt! As the saying goes, "The truth shall set you free."

In Don's case, he conditioned himself to suppress anger when, as a teenager, he was subjected to bearing the wrath of his father. He didn't want to be like his father and swallowed his own anger. A kind-hearted young man, Don believed that is was better to meet the needs of others than to show anger. He wanted to experience love. What Don didn't realize is that accumulated anger has the opposite effect; it blocks love and produces fear.

What's the perceived fear? The fear is that if we express anger, it will prevent us from having the love we so desire from others. This fear, that love is endangered, causes people-pleasing behavior (doing things for others to ensure their love for us). Note that when we go out of our way to people-please or be nice and we don't get the expected love or appreciation back, we get angry. But if there's a habit of suppressing the anger, it will be unconscious. The unexpressed anger triggers more fear and worry about "what else can I do to attract love." Now you're back to square one.

How did Don reclaim his connection to love? By first recognizing that the old pattern isn't working, acting on that truth, and making choices that are authentic, not out of obligation. Doing for others does not guarantee love. Love comes from within. It begins by loving your self enough to tell yourself the truth.

Exercise: Return to Love Meditation

The purpose of this meditation is to transmute and integrate unwelcome feelings, not to get rid of them per se. Remember we don't want to make any feeling WRONG. Realize a feeling just IS (including guilt). We don't have to give it any meaning beyond that.

Clients that employ this meditation have reported feeling lighter, freer, more confident, and less anxious or fearful in any situation. Allow approximately 30 minutes to do this exercise in a quiet place where you will not be disturbed.

Read all of the steps ahead of time. Consider recording this exercise on tape in advance or have a friend read it to you so that you can follow it easily.

1. Sit in a chair with your back straight and your feet flat on the ground. See yourself bathed in a cocoon of healing light and love, starting with the toes and heading up past the top of your head.

2. Focus on your breathing. Consciously inhale fully and exhale normally (without forcing the breath). Connect your breathing by inhaling immediately following each inhalation without pausing. Find a rhythm that is comfortable for you. Do this for a few minutes so that you can do it easily without too much concentration.

3. Notice that you are still bathed in the light of love. Continue with your breath work, and now allow yourself to feel whatever unwelcome feeling you wish to transmute (anger, fear or guilt) so that you can return to love. Realize that this feeling has served you and you are now ready to let it go. Say, "I am willing to return to love."

4. Continue with your connected breathing until you feel you have integrated your feelings. If you are tearful, allow yourself to cry. You are complete when you experience a sense of well-being. Some clients find themselves even smiling or laughing at this stage.

5. Take a moment to jot down what you experienced.

_____

_____

_____

_____

_____

_____

Wonderful! It takes courage to do this work, but the benefits for you and your teens are immeasurable.

How do you know when you are no longer susceptible to guilt? When you make choices that benefit you (honor your true feelings), not only because your choice benefits others (serves their needs).

As you continue on, keep in mind that each feeling is one within the spectrum of human emotions just as the color orange is one of the hues in our color spectrum. We've discussed that you can no more get rid of a feeling by either stuffing or dumping it than you can the color orange. See orange integrating with the other colors to become white. Know that your unwelcome feeling can also integrate into the one light. Light is contained in each feeling. When you give yourself permission to feel it fully, the feeling can move through the light, where it returns to love. It's that simple.

SUMMARY

The underlying message of anger, fear or guilt is a call to experience more love. To experience more love, you need to reclaim your emotional integrity. When you have sufficient love, you can transform unwelcome feelings into compassion, patience, and forgiveness. Those who have successfully walked this path—clearing the three top parenting pitfalls—report that the benefits of living life without baggage from the past, and confidently guiding their children to do the same in the future, far outweigh the initial discomfort.

"For one human to love another
that is perhaps the most difficult of our tasks,
the ultimate test and proof,
the work for which all other work is but preparation."
Rainer Maria Rilke

PART THREE

Seven Simple Steps

CHAPTER 11

#1 Heart Connection

Now that you have paved the way to becoming a parent coach, you are ready to learn tangible coaching skills that establish and sustain trust and closeness as your children move through the inevitable phases of their lives. If you are like most parents, you are both eager to learn new parent coaching techniques and feel that you have a long way to go before you'll be proficient in consistently relating to your teen in new ways. Be patient with yourself and the process. Impatience delays progress. There are four distinct stages to any process of learning something new. Think back to when you first learned to drive a car. Most likely, you were excited about the freedom that driving often brings. One could say your heart was in it. You had the kind of exuberance someone has who doesn't quite know what they don't know.

Soon you realized that driving required practice. You had to concentrate on every little step (putting the key in the ignition, where to put your feet, how to use the mirrors, etc.). It wasn't quite as easy as you had anticipated. You made some mistakes and got somewhat discouraged. But you didn't give up. You kept going because not being able to drive was inconceivable. Take this same level of commitment and apply it to being a great parent coach. Then you will succeed in shifting your relationship and helping your teen build a positive future.

In the next stage, you felt much more comfortable with your new skills. You drove to school, to church, to the mall, under an adult's supervision without any mishaps. Perhaps, you were still unsure of yourself in heavy traffic or at high speeds on the interstate. You continued practicing to maneuver around unexpected situations. Here, too, the more you practice, the better you will get at applying what you've learned to the myriad of challenges parents face with teens.

Finally, after having built a good driving foundation, you graduated. You passed your driver's examination and a new world of driving opened to you. Your practice paid off. You continued to develop safe driving habits on your own to perfect your new skill. And so it is with perfecting your parent coach skills.

Human beings are motivated by moving away from pain or toward pleasure. So whether you want to ease the negativity and tension you are experiencing with teens, or you are focused on helping your teen create a great life, it all begins in the heart. Did you know that in an unborn child, the heart is formed first? According to Dr. Sabina DeVita's presentation at the 2003 *Young Living* conference, this information is available to us from Russia using GDV cameras. What's more the heart starts beating before the brain is formed! After 30 years of research by the HeartMath Institute, the heart is considered to be the true seat of the mind. Researchers report that the heart has its own independent nervous system and that 60-65% of all the cells in the heart are neurons—exactly the same as in the brain. That's significant! Why? Because in our Western culture, we have erroneously believed that the mind is preeminent.

Okay, so what do these scientific facts have to do with coaching teens? To successfully coach teens, we must engage the mind and the heart. According to author Daniel Goleman, we have two different kinds of intelligence: rational and emotional. Success in life is based on our ability to manage our feelings. The heart is our source for emotional intelligence. Information is first accessed by the heart for emotional significance. The heart communicates this to the brain via the thalamus to the amygdala. We feel the information BEFORE we process it. Then, we give it meaning, an interpretation, based on our prior experiences.

Have you ever experienced being misunderstood? Consider this situation that one of my trained coaches shared with me. Karen was listening to Barry, a teen whose father served in the Navy. At one point in his story, Barry began to use foul language for no apparent reason. Karen respectfully made the following request, "I feel uncomfortable with your swearing and ask you to please refrain from using inappropriate language during our talks together." He immediately got very upset and wanted to leave the room. Since no one can know what goes on in another person's head, Karen invited him to tell her what specifically about her message triggered his reaction. Barry was willing to do this because he could feel and hear her heartfelt desire to understand his viewpoint. It turned out that in his experience with his father, the word "inappropriate" was used to indicate that a severe infraction had occurred. Barry had automatically reacted based on his conditioned meaning (personal filter) for this word.

Interestingly, the misunderstanding occurred due to the meaning Barry attached to the word "inappropriate." He wasn't upset about the request to stop swearing, only the use of the word inappropriate. Rather than arguing that the word "inappropriate" in her view was harmless, Karen stayed in her heart space and respected his viewpoint and adjusted her communication to resume communicating effectively. If Karen hadn't maintained her heart connection with this teen upon being challenged regarding her word usage, it's unlikely that she could have easily returned to being in rapport with Barry. It's more likely that her mind would have wanted to defend her position and engage in an argument.

Communication takes place when the message is received and understood. There must be a connection. The point of contact for that connection is the heart. Therefore, in order to become an effective parent coach, you need to begin with establishing a heart connection.

We can all positively impact our communications when we first establish a heartfelt connection between ourselves and others and do our best to sustain it. Why? Because we now know that the brain will entrain with the heart, not the other way around. Those around us will connect with our heart energy and will in effect entrain with us, increasing the level of rapport between us. It behooves us to congruently come from a place of goodwill.

Early in my career, I was a professional recruiter. Whenever I recruited for Sales positions or for people who would have a lot of contact with the public, I favored those candidates with a smile in their voice. It was a distinct competitive advantage. The action of smiling activates the thymus and the thymus gland is connected to the heart. Try it out for yourself. Think about things that cause you to smile and practice smiling from within your heart when you talk with your teen (or anyone); you will notice that others will be much more willing to hear you. We hear not only with our ears, but with our hearts.

Establishing a heart-to-heart connection is key to upgrading your parent-teen relationship. It produces a foundation of mutual trust and respect so that you can show genuine concern for your teen's welfare and future. As a culture, we often define ourselves by our differences. When you stay focused on differences, it's nearly impossible to respect the perceptions of others. Think unity instead. What do you have in common? If all you can think of is that you share being human, that's a good start. When you honor teens with your full attention and regard, you create an inviting, safe, and supportive space for effective coaching. To do this, consciously reach out and feel your heart-to-heart connection with your teen. Practice with the exercise below. If you feel resistance, acknowledge it, and know that this exercise will help you move through your blocks.

If your current relationship has deteriorated to the degree that feeling a heart connection seems too difficult right now, then begin by accessing an appreciative statement about yourself. What do you value about you? Just find one quality (or more, if you like). Restore your own love tank first. If your tank is empty, you won't have it to give to anyone else.

Exercise: Heart-to-Heart Connection

You can do this exercise alone or with a partner—not your teen—in a quiet place. (Do not do this exercise in a moving vehicle). You will be the one to practice making a connection or you can take turns. It is not necessary for your partner to participate, unless this person also has a close relationship with your teen (other family member, etc.), then it would be beneficial. Read through the entire exercise first and then begin.

1. Sit comfortably, facing an empty chair, where you will not be disturbed. (If you are with a partner, sit facing each other at a conversational distance. Have your partner set a timer for five minutes.) Now imagine your teen sitting across from you and place yourself in a meditative or prayerful state. (Your partner can sit in for your teen, if that helps you.)

2. Connect to your teen heart-to-heart by imagining a tube of light, a beautiful shade of green, emanating from your heart and connecting to your teen's heart. Keep your eyes soft and focused on the heart in front of you. This will keep your mind from wandering.

3. Now deepen the connection by focusing on something that you can appreciate about your teen. Select only one thing, something powerful that helps you uplift and honor this precious person in your life. If you are still having trouble

---

making a heart connection, imagine your teen as a sweet infant in your mind's eye.

By seeing the highest good in your teen without any expectations on your part, feel yourself being fully able to connect. If criticisms or negative thoughts surface, don't attempt to stop them. Instead, visualize them as clouds drifting across the sky. Notice how relaxed you feel and how pleasant it feels to be open, receptive, and connected.

4. As you concentrate on your beloved teen, send your loving thoughts through space. Thoughts such as, "I feel good about you," "I love you," or "I am grateful for you." Feel the energy of love flying from your heart to that of your teen. You know that you have successfully completed this exercise when your heart becomes a safe place of trust and reconciliation. Some of you may experience an increased flow of love coming toward you. The heart is the center of your life force energy.

5. This simple exercise might not be easy at first. However, it is a wonderful practice for establishing a foundation for healthy, caring interactions with your teenager. The more you experience this exercise, the better YOU will feel and the stronger your connection will be.

Write down your insights about this experience below. If you did the exercise with a partner, find out what your partner observed about your body language. What did your partner feel? Be sure to capture your thoughts now.

NOTES:

_____

_____

Parents report that they experience their self-protective armor melting, their heart bubbling over with love and compassion, and they return to a peaceful state. Some experience tears of joy. Others feel an integration taking place where anxiety disappears and the heart becomes a fertile soil for new possibilities.

Can you sense that by repeating the above exercise it will be much easier, and at some point automatic, to shift into making immediate and automatic heart connections? It will be as easy as driving a car. When you do, your parenting style will become more open, flexible, and confident.

You know you are making progress with making a heart connection when

- You hold good thoughts and feelings about your teen
- You treat your teen as a well-intentioned individual
- You regularly send loving energy to all your family members
- You feel grateful for having your teen in your life
- You are compassionate and forgiving
- You are highly respectful even when you believe your teen is mistaken
- You stay in rapport and argue less
- You are win/win oriented
- Your teen invites you to spend more time with him or her

CHAPTER 12

#2 Coaching Presence

The next coaching skill is called coaching presence. It is the ability to be fully present, to come with a quiet mind, and be focused on your teen with no distractions. In our hectic world that's becoming more of a challenge. Without focused attention, teens become more anxious or withdraw because they feel that everything else is more important to the parent than they are.

Developing this presence will also cause your communication's style to become more open, flexible, and confident. Additional elements to being present—to ensure quality communications—are letting go of assumptions, judgments, and control. A parent coach does not impose a personal agenda on others. The coach follows the other's lead and is open to whatever emerges. When you are attentive and open, your teen can feel safe to courageously tell you the truth.

With coaching presence you use a friendly tone. It's been said that what you say is not nearly as important as how you make people feel. Others intuitively know by how they feel whether you value or discount them. What are some things that you do (or your teen does) to cause communication to derail? Here are the top six ways to inhibit meaningful communication.

When you:

=> **Control**

- Interrupt
- Finish another's sentences
- Change the subject (diversion)

(**Impact on Receiver**: *"I can't participate in the conversation"*)

=> **Use a guilt strategy**

- Avoid authenticity (in denial)
- Distort emotions (martyrdom)
- Care only about self; you ignore the other person's feelings

(**Impact on Receiver**: *"I feel manipulated"*)

=> **Become ambivalent**

- Give mixed messages
- Ignore your feelings (passive)
- Continue to do tasks while a person is speaking with you

(**Impact on Receiver**: "You don't care")

=> **Make others wrong**

- Refuse to take another's point of view into account
- Attacks; sarcasm; putdowns

- Blames; use of condemning language

(**Impact on Receiver:** "I feel judged")

=> Appear all knowing
- Have all the answers/lecturing/advising
- Make assumptions; defensive
- Monopolize the conversation (closed mind)

(**Impact on Receiver:** *"You're not flexible"*)

=> Act superior
- Ignore (disrespectful)
- Belittle; criticize
- Command; demand

(**Impact on Receiver:** *"You think you are better than me"*)

These attempts to direct the talker limit the discovery of useful information and block understanding. Typically, this "I don't care about you; I care about me" attitude surfaces when the listener doesn't want to hear what is being said, doesn't know how to handle what is being said, assumes they already know what is being said or disagrees with what is being presented. This behavior breeds power struggles or leads to an impasse. It increases stress and undermines rapport and trust. Conversely, encouraging the talker with a coaching presence creates connection and expands information. Ask yourself, "To what extent do I inhibit or encourage communication?"

The communication process is complicated enough without using the above counterproductive tactics. For most people, speaking is like breathing; we do it automatically without spending much time on how we do it. Mostly, we notice how other people are lacking in good communication skills. Observe your communication patterns; in which situations do you curtail communications? There's no need to feel bad about it, just be aware of it. Know that it's okay to stop in mid-sentence, and say, "I don't want to say it like that. Let me begin again."

Let's take a closer look at how communication happens and how it breaks down. First, we have the sender who encodes the message. In deciding to speak to your teenager, you use words to convey what you have in mind. Think about your desired outcome before opening your mouth. Being clear about your purpose can immediately influence how you communicate. The potential for misunderstanding starts here based on your word selection and tone. If your tone is caring, then the words you choose are still important to the message, but they are secondary. If your tone is angry, then even the best selection of words will be contaminated. If you need to send a message to the receiver and you expect that it may not be well received, practice using a tone with a neutral charge; called "charge neutral" in coaching. It takes the emotion out of your words.

For harmonious communication to occur, you need to be in rapport. It's the most important ingredient to any interaction. You do it naturally when there is a sense of shared understanding; when that's not there, find something likable in the other person. Make a heart-to-heart connection. Each of us has traits that attract or repel. To develop rapport, be an attraction finder, not a fault finder.

To get additional feedback about how you sound, ask an objective adult whom you can trust to be truthful with you. Ask: Do I speak in a way that invites open conversation? Does my tone reflect lightness and a positive orientation or do I sound tense and impatient? How much do I allow the strong emotions of others to influence me and how well do I manage my own emotions? Now back to our communication's model.

Next the receiver decodes the message. This means the receiver, your teen, interprets the message based on his or her own experience base, personal knowledge, filters of the world, and emotional state. If the sender and receiver have different assumptions, vocabulary, and communication styles, there's a good chance that the message will be decoded differently from the sender's intent, just as in the example shared in an earlier chapter, where the young man got triggered after hearing the word "inappropriate."

Then, the receiver transmits feedback to the sender. The words the sender selects often provides clues about how he or she interpreted the message. At the end of the conversation, it's a good idea to check for understanding to avoid making assumptions. Looking at this communications model, isn't it a wonder we understand each other at all?

To succeed at communicating, recognize that communication takes place when we allow for individual differences and when your message has been received and acknowledged. Some of the time, others will agree with us and sometimes, not. Too often we think successfully communicating means that we've converted the other to our way of thinking. You are successful when you respectfully and truthfully deliver your message for another's consideration. You can tell when you are being manipulative because your sole concern will be getting your own way without regard for the other person. Just because teens inhabit young bodies doesn't give adults license to be forceful, rigid or dogmatic. Treat them as you would one of your closest friends. Give them adult-like respect.

A frequent complaint from parents is that they can't get their kids to help with household chores without a fight. When I probe further, I find (a) that parents assign tasks unilaterally without providing reasonable choices, (b) that parents language their requests without gaining a clear agreement, and (c) that there are no provisions for consequences in the event of broken agreements.

Let's look at this example. A client named Linda, a career woman and a single parent, became frustrated when both of her preteens refused to clear the dinner table and place the dishes in the dishwasher. Without any previous discussion or agreement, she said after dinner, "I'd like both of you to take care of the dishes." They responded that they didn't want to do it and simply left the table. The same thing happened the next evening.

At my suggestion, Linda demonstrated a coaching presence by creating a list of tasks around the house that could be divided up between herself and her children. She then met with them, explained the need for the family to work together to keep their home neat, outlined her expectations for each task, and let them choose which three they would each prefer to do. By providing reasonable choices instead of commanding them, there was no more resistance by the children to do their share. Linda completed this discussion by asking her kids for their ideas about reasonable consequences in order to keep them all accountable. Done! No more vagueness, no more disappointment. Plus, the relationship between mom and her teens was strengthened as they each learned to be there for each other.

In communicating with other adults at home or at the office, most of us have learned to make clear requests and form specific agreements. Why not teach your children this very important life skill early?

Another parent, Ann, agreed to help her 19-year-old son with a college project. She promised to meet him at the library twice a week for four weeks at 5 PM. At the office, she set a timer for 4:30, but couldn't get herself to leave the office to be on time for her meeting with her son. The first few times it happened, her son sat there patiently waiting for Ann. She apologized to him and vowed she'd do better. Finally, HE didn't show up. That's when she clearly realized that "do as I say, not as I do" doesn't work and isn't right. As the parent, it is her responsibility to be a good role model for her son. Now they both keep each other honest.

When your coaching presence includes fully accepting your own humanness, you will admit your mistakes, thus creating a zone of safety. By accepting your own faults and talents, you open the door for others to have the same experience of themselves. You'll have an aura of "I'm okay, you're okay" and others will pick up on your cue. They may not be conscious of the reason they are feeling more comfortable with themselves, but they'll want to be in your presence. You can positively impact others to the degree that you are self-secure.

Exercise

In developing your coaching presence, you will become more aware of your ability to choose the tone for your communications and how to respond to another. You take responsibility for how you conduct yourself. You no longer react to others; instead you choose your thoughts, emotions, and behaviors that are in alignment with the goal to communicate effectively.

1. Recall an example of where your parent-teen communication broke down. See the incident in your mind by imagining that you are seated in a movie theater and you are watching yourself and your teen communicate from a distance.

2. From this perspective, what do you observe on the movie screen in your mind? Are you maintaining a coaching presence or are you allowing your emotions to interfere? What tone is being used? Is it respectful? Are you or your teen engaging in any of the communication inhibitors outlined in this chapter? Write down what you think contributed to the breakdown in communication in this incident. Include specific words that were said.

_____

_____

_____

_____

3. How did your response to the communication breakdown make the problem better or worse? Why? How did you feel?

_____

_____

_____

_____

4. What could you have done to positively impact communication? Write down your preferred response.

_____

_____

_____

_____

_____

5. Now quickly rewind the movie in your head. See it running backwards on the screen in front of you. Notice how goofy it looks. Before you rerun the movie, insert your new effective response. Play the movie on the screen of your mind with the substitution in place. Do this now. How do you feel? If you are not happy with your revised response, try it again until you are. If you are satisfied, go to step six now.

NOTES:

_____

_____

_____

_____

_____

6. Wonderful! Now when you run your movie, step into it. (You are no longer observing; you are acting in it.) Practice experiencing yourself using positive communication at least three more times. Repetition is the key to accelerated learning.

If you are still having trouble shifting your communications style, don't worry. Just be willing. There's more opportunity to learn in the next chapter.

"Accept your children as perfect, as whole, and treat them as though they already are what they can become..."

Dr. Wayne Dyer

You know you are making progress with having a coaching presence when

- You are calm, collected, and fully present
- You are warm, open, and respectful
- You share with your teen without speaking at him or her
- You relate as an equal—not as superior
- You are caring but not overly concerned
- You are flexible—not rigid
- You facilitate what is, not what you think it ought to be
- You accept your humanness and admit your mistakes
- You are spontaneous and trust your intuition
- You treat them as if they are what they can become and coach them based on where they are now

CHAPTER 13

#3 Conscious Listening

Once you can easily connect with your heart (love and compassion) and you embody a coaching presence (open and respectful), you can move beyond yourself to become more consciously aware of others. In coaching, the emphasis is off of yourself and on your teen. Conscious listening is the ability to focus fully on what the other is saying and feeling, honoring unique ideas and experiences. Instead of listening in order to respond, listen to clarify and support. To effectively interact with your teen, your spouse or anyone, it can't be forced by making yourself use a structured technique. Others can sense what you are doing and feel manipulated. If you want someone to open up to you, be genuinely interested and express empathy. Do you share your inner most thoughts right away? Of course not! Self-disclosure occurs when you feel safe.

By cultivating an attitude of curiosity, you bring more openness and a sense of wonder to your interactions. You listen for the purpose of learning. Here you are able to integrate multiple sources of information; you listen with your heart, not just your ears, to gather information beyond what is being said. You listen for feelings, meaning, and behavior. Finding out what lies beneath the words, strengthens your parent-teen connection. You further demonstrate that you care about (respect) the other person by hearing his or her story for the purpose of discovering useful information, not to determine who is right or wrong.

Most people think listening means solving problems or coming up with an answer. If that's your belief, then you will curtail the conversation prematurely. As a listener, you put your own agenda and concerns temporarily on hold. To listen attentively, encourage the talker to share their thoughts without interference; this means you need to be patient and postpone your questions. Most people think they already have all the information they need and want to jump into the conversation. I did this early on with my teens when I was still unwittingly replicating my parents listening pattern. Big mistake! Have you ever had someone trample on your words in mid-sentence? How did you feel? Slow down. Take the time to listen; you're worth it and so is your kid. There is nothing more validating than having someone totally focused on you. So make a conscious decision to listen deeply. To start, practice listening twice as long as you normally do.

Think of a time when you called a friend just to talk about an experience at home or at the office. Then, as your friend patiently listens to your description of what happened and how you felt about it, suddenly the solution presented itself. How do you feel when another guides you to solving a vexing problem? All of us can benefit from processing our experiences by talking out loud, when the listener makes it safe for us to do so. When you give the gift of consciously listening, kids can listen to themselves and make sense of their situation. It empowers them and fosters self-reliance. Don't rob your child from having these opportunities.

Further it gives you valuable insights into their thinking processes, beliefs, values, and worldview. Parents often ask me, "Can you help me get into my teen's head?" Giving your kids space to talk out loud, and listening with respect, is a great way to discover what they're thinking. Plus it contributes to your teen's feelings of being loved and accepted. Compare how this feels to having someone disturb your story by interrupting or insisting on giving you advice. Does how you listen help or hinder the conversation?

The number one complaint I hear from teenagers and parents alike is that they don't feel heard. When you feel heard, the level of trust and safety in the relationship magnifies. As the leader and parent coach, take the initiative to learn conscious listening. The better you are at modeling this important skill to your kids, the easier it will be for them to follow. Remember our earlier discussion about how all children have a built-in camcorder; everything you've ever said and done has been recorded. Eventually, they will play it back to you, often much to our chagrin.

How you listen affects the *quality* of the information *you receive*. Here are seven powerful ways to enhance your ability to listen.

1. **Make and maintain eye contact.**

   Focus on your teen. This will keep your mind from wandering and conveys your full attention. Position yourself so that you can make eye-to-eye contact. (If you hear something that you don't like or doesn't make sense, avoid the temptation to roll your eyes.)

2. **Stop what you are doing.**

   The best time to talk with your teen is when he or she approaches you although this may not always be possible. Multitasking is not an option; it's too distracting. If you are doing something that already has your full attention, change gears and give your undivided attention to your teen. If that's not possible right away, because you are already speaking with someone else or you are in the middle of an important task, then give yourself the opportunity to finish what you are doing by saying something like this, "I want to talk with you, too, and in order to give you my full attention. I'll be done in 15 minutes and then I'll be able to listen to you. Okay?" Most everyone will honor this positive approach.

3. **Have a breath (one or more!).**
To help you shift gears and clear your mind from your thoughts and your previous activity, take a full but silent breath and connect to your teen with your heart. If you have been practicing this, you can easily access appreciation and compassion. Now you will be able to travel into the talker's world and be more prepared to comprehend the situation as he or she is experiencing it. Then listen with your body and your mind.

4. **Attend to the talker.**
Instead of listening for a pause to insert your opinion, be curious. Ask yourself, "What thoughts and feelings can I identify?" Is my teen enthusiastic and hopeful or disappointed and overwhelmed? Listen for the talker's concerns, values, and beliefs. Observe their words, tone of voice, and body language. Most people have a tendency to only partially hear the talker, because they are more intent on mentally rehearsing what they are going to say next. Wait. Use your coaching presence skills to fully take in what the other is saying.

5. **Acknowledge the talker's experience.**

Acknowledgements allow you to confirm the words you are hearing to deepen the communication. A simple empathic acknowledgement, such as "Hmm," "I see," "Uh huh," a nod or a smile let's the talker know that you are listening. To show respect and acceptance, but not necessarily agreement, of what the talker is saying reflect back what you think you heard. Whenever possible use the same words that the talker used without sounding mechanical. Everyone likes to be quoted.

Summarizing builds trust in the relationship; however, too much paraphrasing leads to inaccuracies. Reflect back parts of the conversation as the talker speaks. "This is really important to you." "It sounds like you are changing your mind." "It's a big decision." Then, confirm your findings, say "Have I got it right?" "Is this correct?"

6. **Reflect the talker's feeling with empathy.**

   To create a closer connection between yourself and your teen, pay particular attention to and verbalize the feeling, not just the words, of the message you are hearing. "It sounds like you are feeling nervous about your upcoming exam." "You sound excited about your new friend." "You feel disappointed because you believe I let you down." To do this well, you will need to go with, not against, the talker's experience. The purpose is to acknowledge and build rapport, not to indulge in knee-jerk reactions or attempt to change the feeling or experience. Saying something like, "You don't really feel that" because it's not how you are experiencing the same situation only serves to block and shut down communication. (Caution: do not overuse this reflecting technique after every sentence; it's annoying and inhibits the spontaneous flow of conversation.)

   Use the statement "I understand" sparingly. First, we can never exactly understand how someone else is experiencing something. Second, it is often misused when the listener wants to take charge of the conversation. Third, know that it is not necessary to understand or agree with your teen. It's more important to demonstrate your WILLINGNESS to understand by acknowledging or validating what you are hearing. Your job as parent coach is to listen to learn more about your teen and the situation at hand. You want your teen to feel "gotten." Check for accuracy; don't assume you've got it right. If you are kinesthetic, you'll know when you've got the essence of what your teen is saying because an energy shift will occur. You will feel being in accord. Acknowledging also serves to help the talker clarify feelings. As a result, your teen might surprise you by expressing his or her gratitude. Yes, really!

7. **Be patient; refuse to interrupt.**

Attending and acknowledging demonstrates to your teen that you care. It leads to connection and cooperation. To follow the talker's story without sidetracking, don't interrupt, no matter how tempting it is. I'm not going to tell you that this is easy. It isn't. As one parent said, "It takes everything in me to let my son talk and to listen." The more you practice, the better you will get. If it's a complicated or emotionally charged conversation, take notes to stay calm and keep track of your own thoughts, questions, ideas, and concerns. Remember your objective right now is to listen, summarize, and mirror back what the talker said to promote clarity, caring, and connection. You may or may not always understand your teen, but this does not have to limit your love.

The purpose of conscious listening is to gather more information so that you can go beyond surface issues, keep from getting hooked by your teen's story, and reach informational gold. Build trust and strengthen your connection by helping the talker feel comfortable sharing with you. Below are some simple ways to invite the talker to continue with whatever he or she is willing to tell you that suggests "I am here to listen to you; keep talking." It is particularly important to encourage the talker to keep speaking when you feel the urge to interrupt in order to defend, disagree or give unsolicited advice.

Gently and lightly say,

"Tell me more."
"Is there anything else?"
"Would you like to add anything else?"
"This is hard for me to hear, but please continue."

Encouraging another to speak several times after he or she says there is nothing more to add, provides the talker with freedom to reveal richer information. This technique is much more efficient than playing a guessing game of asking 20 questions.

Are there occasions when you need to interrupt or redirect? Yes, there are a few exceptions. One client's daughter, Kathy, is a "babbling brook." Kathy loves to talk. She freely expresses everything she sees, hears, and feels. Her mother needs to call periodic time-outs, because listening to Kathy for two hours straight is unproductive and exhausting. (Mom can't sustain her focus.) When you feel that you can no longer listen, you need to be honest and say so. Do not pretend to be listening. It's not fair to you or the talker.

In another situation, Robert, told me that he had been blasted by this 18-year-old daughter. Meg accused him of being a bad parent. He allowed her to vent at first, but soon it was obvious that Meg's purpose was to dump all her anger on him. Robert felt like someone had just vomited on him. His heart began to pound wildly, and he knew he needed to take responsibility for managing his emotions. So he interrupted Meg to let her know that if she continued to carry on in this fashion, he would need to end the call and suggested another time to continue their conversation—giving both of them an opportunity to calm down. Feeling even more slighted now she ignored his attempt to schedule another time to talk with her later that day.

Robert wisely terminated the call since there was no reasoning with Meg now. And he didn't want to risk any further alienation. Robert successfully managed this situation and enforced his boundary. Listening respectfully applies both ways. They talked a few days later, when Meg was in a better mood and able to listen, and they had a pleasant conversation.

In the workplace, customer service representatives are trained to let an irate customer vent; however, if the customer doesn't calm down and crosses the line (swear words or foul language), the representatives are given the green light to terminate the conversation. No one deserves to be verbally mistreated. This applies to the office or in the home. Don't hesitate to call a time-out. A parent coach models appropriate listening and speaking skills. Better your kids learn it from you now than to have to send them to anger management classes later.

How do you and your teen benefit from conscious listening:

- Allows you to more effectively relate and respond to your teen's concerns
- Expedites getting to the core of the issue or situation
- Establishes a collaborative environment for negotiating agreements
- Creates a greater willingness for your teen to listen to you when it's your turn to speak
- Causes your teen to feel good about you which increases trust and enhances your relationship
- Coaches your teen to become a great listener
- Motivates your teen to seek your counsel

Exercise

A. List five ways you can demonstrate conscious listening:

1 _____

2 _____

3 _____

4 _____

5 _____

Super! Now it's time to practice.

B Fieldwork:

Schedule some quality time, conducive to talking, one-to-one with each teen (separate from meal times with the rest of the family). Tell him or her that you want to be able to listen better. Ask if he or she would be willing to help you learn. Let your kid know well in advance so that you can both clear your schedules and stay free from distractions. Let your teen choose the topics. Have your teen signal you when you step into old patterns. Get creative. One parent let his kid wave a penalty flag every time he started giving advice or rolling his eyes. Keep track of your results below:

NOTES

_____

_____

_____

_____

_____

Congratulations on completing your fieldwork. If you are still not totally convinced about how important it is to "Just Listen," here is a quote from an article written by Daniel S. Levy (source *Time* Magazine; May 31, 1999, page 103):

"The State of Washington's Children study reports that children are far less likely to engage in risky behavior like getting pregnant, dropping out of school or selling drugs if they feel they have the opportunity to share their views with a trusted adult. One way many savvy adults bond with their kids is by turning off the radio (while driving) and drawing them into conversation during those long drives from school to sports practice or to a piano recital."

Conscious listening not only provides you more accurate data about what your teen is experiencing, it also serves to affirm his or her intrinsic worth. Each of us longs (and deserves) to be accepted, heard, and acknowledged. Empathic conscious listening honors kids on a deep level, opening and nurturing their God-given gifts and talents.

Instead of listening for a pause to insert your opinion, practice listening for what's admirable about the speaker. Pay attention to his or her gifts, traits, and talents, and take a moment to point them out. How would that impact your relationships? By taking your neediness out of the loop, you'll find that others are much more willing to listen to you and support you when you are the one who is speaking. As client Greg said, "Listening carefully and not reacting creates a safe place for my 17-year-old daughter to express herself. Then helping her navigate through options and explore possibilities is possible. Coaching is a powerful way to build respectful relationships with teenagers." When parents set their intention to honor their children in this way, young people learn to do this for themselves and for each other.

"Role modeling is the most basic responsibility of parents. They are handing life's scripts to their children, scripts that in all likelihood will be acted out much of the rest of the children's lives."

Stephen R. Covey

You know you are making progress with conscious listening when

- You listen with your deepest self
- You hear and feel what is behind the information you are given (values, beliefs, concerns)
- You listen for the purpose of learning more
- You listen patiently instead of preparing your response
- You accept what is being said without reacting negatively
- You invite your teen to say more instead of hijacking the conversation
- You stay with the talker's agenda
- You follow the conversation and respond to what has just been said
- You mirror back what was said, summarize, and check for accuracy
- You experience the world through your teen's eyes
- Your teen exhibits great listening skills

CHAPTER 14

#4 *Insightful Questioning*

So far, you've learned to enhance your parent-teen relationship by sustaining a heart-to-heart connection, being flexible and open, and listening that allows you to accurately comprehend and summarize the essence of your teen's message. Keep in mind that your job is not to figure out your teen. We cannot know what another person is fully feeling and experiencing. When you hear something that is particularly puzzling or challenging, stand back, stay calm, and be in the present. Memories of the past or worries of the future get in the way of being alert and aware. Before you can express thoughts that are useful and meaningful, you need to ask insightful questions. Be willing to dance in the moment and to not have all the answers. Create a space for additional information to emerge. Confer with your inner intelligence, your intuition.

The purpose of learning to ask insightful questions is to support the development of an honest and authentic relationship between your teen and you. Ultimately, it also leads to a satisfying relationship between your teen and the world. In this chapter, you will be given an "essential questions" toolkit.

Insightful questions can focus conversation and are useful for evoking insights, discovery, and possibility. Questions that lead to greater clarity, awareness, or new learning are nearly always open-ended questions. Asking closed questions generally limit responses to "yes," "no," or "whatever." A typical parental closed question is, "Did you do your homework?" What would happen if instead you asked, "How much homework do you have today? How's your homework coming along? What can you do to ensure that your homework will be done on time? How can I support you in doing your homework?" Experiment with open questions that begin with "Who," "What," "Where," "When," "How," and, "Why." The usefulness of a question is determined by the quality of information it produces. Parents report that open-ended questions yield rich results.

In part one of this book, you learned first hand how using the power of positive why can help you move toward a desired goal. Let's also make a distinction between curious "why" questions a four-year old asks (Why is the sky blue?) and "why" questions an adult asks that produces needless tension ("Why isn't your room clean yet?"). The latter evokes a need to justify the action or behavior. Drop the "why" for less defensiveness. Why leads to separation, not connection. Be very discerning about using "why" questions.

One of the easiest ways to practice using open-ended questions, is to begin with "What." Let's say your teen is explaining a situation; however, you sense there may be something else she isn't sharing. How could you ask an insightful question using "what" that reflects your conscious listening ability and your understanding of your teen's perspective? Remember you still don't have the complete story. You could non-judgmentally and with a charge neutral tone say, "I heard you say that you're upset because your teacher accused you of cheating in front of the entire class today. You're angry to have been accused and even more furious that it was done in front of your classmates. That was insensitive of him and must have been very uncomfortable for you... and I sense there is something else here. What else happened?" When you use these words and you are congruent with your message (your tone and body language is sincere and nonjudgmental), you create an opportunity for honest sharing.

Other essential "what" questions that can deepen awareness and learning that might be useful in this situation are, "What might you do differently the next time around given the same circumstances?" "What is likely to happen if you don't address this issue?" "What are you in control of in this situation?" "What do you intend to do going forward?" "What would you like to have happen now?" "What is the worst that could happen? "What is the first thing you need to do now?" and so on. Ask questions one at a time; no barrage of questions, please. Provide for sufficient time to get a meaningful answer. Many people wait less than two seconds for the answer, before they jump back in with a comment or another question. Do whatever it takes to train yourself to wait (count to 10, put your hand over your mouth, focus on your breathing, etc.).

Judy has a 17-year-old daughter, Denise, who felt frustrated and misunderstood by one of her teachers. It was clear to me that Denise and her teacher had very different communications styles. The girl found her style to be stifling. Denise often shutdown and was unwilling to speak out, to ask questions or openly share her ideas; she feared that she would be seen as noncompliant. To help her daughter get out of her poor me trap, Judy asked "what" questions: "What can you do to let go of your disappointment about this teacher? What good can come from this situation? What are you in control of? What would happen if you focused on acknowledging your abilities (your natural curiosity and ability to ask provocative questions) instead of how you want your teacher to be different? What is likely to happen if you allow this teacher to turn you off from learning?" Soon Denise refused to let herself be negatively impacted by this authority figure. With her mother's loving support, Denise could appreciate who she is, value her abilities, and know her worth without needing this particular teacher's approval. Denise learned that what others think does not have to determine her behavior. She can choose to say "yes" to herself.

My client Rita beautifully handled a situation with her 16-year-old son who announced that he wanted to move out of the house and get his own place. Instead of responding, "That's ridiculous. You don't have a job and can't afford an apartment," Rita inquired, "What kind of apartment are you looking to rent?" After he described it to her she acknowledged that it sounded nice and continued with "how much rent will you need to pay?" He didn't have a clue, so she asked him, "How will you go about getting that information?" At this point, it was clear to him that he didn't have a plan and he didn't know what to do next. Rita offered, "Would you like me to help you create a plan?" Her son gladly accepted her help and together they gathered the data for rent, utilities, and other related expenses. Afterwards, her son decided that he couldn't afford to move out and remained at home.

Rita was elated at the news because she really didn't want him to leave; she felt he was much too young. Rita stayed focused on her son's agenda, not her own. She was grateful that she hadn't tried to command or convince him to stay home. It was much more rewarding for her and empowering for him to allow him to come to the same conclusion on his own!

Paul has a teenage daughter who has a habit of complaining: about school, about her friends, about life. Paul first respectfully gives her his full attention and allows her to vent about a new situation without judgment. Thereafter, when he has a good grasp of the situation and just before she begins to sound like a broken record, he asks, "How are you contributing to this situation? How does it feel when you stay in this complaint mode? How could you respond differently?"

Occasionally teens have trouble answering; they can't see the forest for the trees. At this point, Paul has learned to ask his daughter if it would be all right if he shares his perspective on her situation. If she says "Yes," he offers his thoughts and ideas. If she says, "Not really," then the conversation is over for now. Another opportunity will follow. Paul has learned to honor her preference without feeling rejected or trying to convince her otherwise. If a parent has been listening well and has acknowledged the teen's view, then the probability is very high that the teenager will be equally as open to hearing your views. Note that you are complete with this communication, after you have shared your perspective, whether your child agrees with it or not.

Some parents initially find the idea of asking permission to share their opinions distasteful. They believe that as a parent they have the freedom to speak their mind. Of course you do AND the listener has the freedom to listen or tune you out. Have you ever tuned anyone out? What happens when you deliver a lecture to your kid? When you engage in a monologue, how much listening takes place? Not much, if any. It's not about having the right to speak; it's about creating an atmosphere for listening so that what you are saying has a chance to be heard. When your teen says, "Yes," an inner shift takes place that allows for more listening to take place. Every individual, including your offspring, has a choice to listen or not listen. When you ask permission, your teen feels loved and respected, enhancing your relationship—the wish of every parent. You can have your wish come true, when you are willing to let go of what you have done in the past and learn new effective parent coach patterns of communicating.

Exercise

Learning to be a parent coach is about asking insightful questions, not handing out the right answer. Your role is to be a valuable, gentle guide so that young people can learn to access their own answers.

A. Practice crafting open ended "what" questions. To make them more meaningful for you, think about a situation you encountered recently with your teen. In doing so, you will be prepared to use your new questioning skill at the next opportunity.

---

1 _____

2 _____

3 _____

4 _____

5 _____

6 _____

7 _____

8 _____

9 _____

10 _____

You don't need to stop here. One client developed categories for a variety of conversation topics. In no time, she arrived at 101 insightful "what" questions.

B. Now do this same exercise for "how" questions.

1 _____

2 _____

3 _____

4 _____

5 _____

6 _____

7 _____

8 _____

9 _____

10 _____

Practice using these questions. Asking what and how questions will help you (and your teen) learn more about the motivation that lies behind the desire. You can use insightful questioning for any situation, whether your teenager wants to quit sports, avoid a friend, get a job, buy a skateboard, change her diet or get his body pierced. It will give you the information that lies beneath their requests and will keep you from automatically criticizing them for wanting something that may not make sense to you. The more you can stay calm and explore possibilities, the more your teenager will talk with you openly, instead of secretly getting what they want behind your back.

SPECIAL OFFER: Contact us at www.teenfrontier.com and request our free list of powerful and insightful questions.

There's no need to wait for conflict to arise to benefit from asking insightful questions. To enjoy quality time sharing with your teen on a daily basis for the purpose of deepening your relationship, without problem-solving, reflect on what you can do to add more intimacy. (Intimacy is defined as "a mutual and spontaneous expression of feelings, thoughts or beliefs.") How can you get to know each other better? A conversation starter could be, "I don't know if I ever really enjoyed (fill in the blank). Where are you with that?" This approach opens the door for you to invite more intimacy and to share a piece of yourself. Age appropriate self-disclosure enhances parent-teen relationships. For additional ideas on developing curiosity and intimacy, refer to the Conversation Deepeners in Appendix 4.

Soon you, too, will be able to experience what John did, "I had lunch with my daughter and this time I was able to fully enjoy our conversation. All I did was listen to her and ask questions. It was delightful for me and she got a lot out of it as well. It was amazing!"

"...curiosity is an important part of being successful because that is what drives someone to think a little harder, do a little more.
    Karin Ireland

You know you are making progress with insightful questioning when

- You are relaxed and receptive to knowing more
- Your questions reflect the needs and interests of your teen
- Your open-ended questions produce greater clarity
- Your questions help your teen access possibilities and solutions
- You use your intuition to customize your questions
- You notice how well your teen is absorbing information without pushing or lecturing
- You use their phrasing whenever possible
- You are attentive without being intrusive
- You clarify what was said or meant
- You ask questions that move your teen toward learning more about themselves and what they want to accomplish
- You stop lecturing or nagging and start coaching
- You experience enhanced relationships

CHAPTER 15

#5 Affirming Words

Taking the time to praise your kids can yield huge benefits, especially if you focus on meaningful acknowledgments, not just a generic "good job." Keep your focus on the inherent uniqueness of each child. Say, "I really appreciate your enthusiasm for sports (music or learning)." Or, "I noticed how much effort you put into making sure the lawn looks great." Such affirming words will help teens get more in touch with their attributes and help them appreciate who they really are. It helps them know their talents and develop their strengths: the key to fulfilling achievement and coaching your teen to success. With frequent doses of sincere appreciation, kids are more likely to relax, accept themselves, and let go of am-I-good-enough concerns that many adults still face.

Our parents were raised in an era where giving praise was limited to young children. Once a child transitioned into adolescence, criticisms replaced praise. Parents bragged about their kids to other parents, but neglected to affirm their own kid for fear of giving him or her "a big head." Parents then held the belief that they could far better motivate and mold teens by pointing out that there is always more to attain. Nothing is further from the truth. In the office and in the home the emphasis has shifted to reinforcing positive behavior with affirming words, not harping on weaknesses. Critical and harsh words are harmful to all of us, especially kids. More than any other stage, teens are vulnerable. In searching for their identity, they compare themselves to others and often conclude that they don't fit or measure up. When this happens, self worth plummets.

Many of us intuitively know that words are powerful; they can encourage or discourage. Dr. Masaru Emoto from Japan offered the world breakthrough scientific evidence in his Messages From Water series; the first volume was published in June 1999. Dr. Emoto wrapped words around bottles containing water and froze the water. He then captured the resulting crystalline structure of each of the water samples on camera. How water "responded" to these words, ranging from "you fool" to "a happy home," was remarkable. The two words that had the most impact in transforming water into beautiful crystals were: *love* and *thank you* (appreciation). Harsh and discouraging words, as in "I will kill you" or "You make me sick," resulted in crystals that looked weak, disconnected, and in some cases even annihilated. Identical experiments were done using the same words in different languages, not just English and Japanese, with consistent findings. Don't just take my word for it. I highly recommend you look at Dr. Emoto's photo collection yourself. It is truly indescribable. Consider viewing Dr. Emoto's crystalline structures with your entire family. The author summarizes his discoveries with these words "Words are the vibrations of nature. Therefore beautiful words create beautiful nature. Ugly words create ugly nature..." As humans, our beauty is most apparent when we are happy and satisfied with ourselves. Teach your children about happiness from within. Provide them with positive and loving messages about their uniqueness.

Words that affirm encourage. You encourage someone when you recognize an individual's inherent value and you accept him or her unconditionally. You demonstrate encouragement when you verbally affirm those aspects of behavior that you can genuinely appreciate, without waiting for perfection. Positively recognizing effort, contributions, and progress increases a sense of worth and confidence. Critical reminders that your teen is not yet meeting your expectations tends to discourage and leads to a feeling of inadequacy. Words that negate range from the harsh "No, do it this way, stupid!" to the more subtle "Here, let me do it for you (sigh)."

Making critical statements to ourselves, our kids, and even the television often happens automatically, unconsciously. Become aware of your inner critical monologue. When you pass a stranger on the street, what do you hear yourself saying? What comments pop into your head about someone's appearance or behavior? Are they encouraging or critical? How about when you watch sports? Do you second-guess the players, get irritated, and comment on what they should've done? If that's the default software program you are running in your computer-mind, then it will automatically engage when you are with your teens. Think about it. After your kid has mowed the lawn, washed the car or cooked a meal, is your first inclination to point out what wasn't perfect about it or do you express your appreciation for the positive effort?

If you are someone who falls into the automatically critical camp, it's time to install a new preferred software program (affirming words) in your brain. There's no need to uninstall your old program. What happens when you try to uninstall a computer program? In most cases, the program is so fragmented that it's nearly impossible to delete all of the pieces. Simply install the new parent coach program and consciously access affirming words. The new program, when engaged repetitively, will generate new preferred results effortlessly. For all practical purposes, the old program ceases to exist.

Here are some words you can begin using immediately that encourage a young person while he or she is developing a skill (i.e., writing a report, giving a presentation, learning a foreign language):

- It looks as if you worked hard on that; how do you think you did?

- Everyone makes mistakes; what will you do differently next time?

- I know you are disappointed about not being further along; do you have any idea how FAR you've come?

- You can do it.

Client Denise complained to me about her ex-husband's critical approach with their son. Jonathan is 11 years old, loves sports above all else, and he's quite good at it. He plays soccer on the same team that his father coaches. Dad expects more from his son than he does from the other boys and continues his criticisms after the game in the car on the way home. Denise attends most of the games and says that her son is a top player, but her husband rarely gives him any credit. The feedback dad gives is unsolicited and harsh. Instead of saying, "Those two goals you scored were awesome, you really helped us win this game," dad rags on Jonathan for the opportunities he missed. It's turning the boy off from playing soccer and more importantly has created lots of distance between father and son.

No matter how good or bad the performance, effort needs to be rewarded. After having played soccer for hours, that is not the time to harp on technique. It will just cause someone to want to give up the sport. Providing corrective feedback is a matter of timing. Giving praise immediately following the game, creates much more openness for instruction prior to the next one.

Denise is going it alone. Her ex-husband doesn't understand why Jonathan prefers mom's company and stubbornly refuses to listen to her explanations of parent coaching. Denise has embraced being a solo parent coach and is learning to give encouraging yet honest feedback.

Denise knows she has no control over her ex and is committed to positively impact her son's life right now without her ex's support. Leading by example can eventually prompt the other parent to join in later.

Of course, it's also important to provide affirming words about your kid's natural talents and traits, not just for performance.

- I know that when you give me your word, I can count on it
- You are so good at making friends
- You always seem to know what soothing words to say to your sister
- I admire your creative mind.

Pam, a mother of two teenage boys, learned to appreciate and celebrate the differences in her younger son. "My relationship with my son is 100% better! Due to your coaching, I am now able to see my son for who he is, and appreciate his special talents. I realize that just because Kye is not like me, his brother or his Dad, does not make him a bad person. In fact, I now look at his personality, and wish I had more of his sense of adventure and his ability to connect with people."

Last, but not least, here are some sample words to express verbal affection to your teen, in addition to traditional "I love you":

- You're wonderful
- I'm grateful you are my son/daughter
- I enjoy you
- Your smile brightens my day.

Variety is important; otherwise, you begin to sound too mechanical. Teens look to adults to have integrity. Come from your heart, not a book. Learn from the examples above and create your own affirming words. Write them on an index card and carry them with you. Make sure you affirm your kid at least once a day. Do you think it's possible to receive too much appreciation? Appreciation is like money; you can never have too much of it. Be aware that if you are using the same language you used when your teen was a child, then it's time to change. Let your affirming words reflect your teen's level of maturity. Maybe it's also time to start calling your son "Bob" instead of "Bobby"? Ask him what he prefers.

Exercise: From Criticizing to Affirming

A. Spend time with your teen and quietly observe what you are thinking as you watch him or her. If you notice critical statements, write them down. Then, reinterpret what you are seeing. Focus on the goodness within. As you focus on loving thoughts about your teen, you experience harmony within your family.

Here's an example. Let's say your kid is listening to music that you don't enjoy. Your thoughts might be, "That's not music, that's noise." The more you criticize your teen's taste in music, the more the teen will feel unloved and unsupported, creating separation. Your disapproval will not cause teens to stop listening to their music. Do you have to learn to like the music? No. Do you need to listen to it? No. Can you still affirm your teen? Yes. You can remind yourself that you listened to music that was different from what your parents liked and you turned out okay. How would it be if you said, "I love you even though I don't appreciate the music you enjoy"?

Or, maybe you believe your daughter is using her cell phone too much to talk with her friends. You could say to yourself, "I can appreciate that my daughter values her friends and likes to stay connected to them."

Perhaps, you think that the hair style or color your kid likes is ugly. What if you change that thought to "I admire the courage my kid has to experiment with what I consider to be a radical style"?

If you have been practicing the previous coaching skills, it will be relatively easy for you to do this exercise. For some of you, making these kinds of shifts will be a stretch. Know that teens will express their individuality and independence regardless of your opinions; however, the quality of your relationship will be determined by how flexible you can be. Take time now to list your big and small criticisms and practice your affirming words. Begin with at least three examples of your own. Record your thoughts and reinterpretations here.

_____

_____

_____

_____

_____

_____

_____

IMPORTANT: Don't be concerned if you are not seeing immediate results. It might take you longer than you thought to shift your focus and cultivate using affirming words. It could also take time for your teen to adjust to the new you. Once you demonstrate that praising and encouraging is your new SOP (standard operating procedure), miracles can happen. Don't make the mistake of giving up on your goal to have a great relationship with your teen. Acknowledge your disappointment to yourself and then support yourself in learning this parent- teen coaching skill by holding positive thoughts about your teen and visualizing already enjoying a harmonious relationship.

B. Every week think of three things that you can appreciate about each member of your family. Write it down and tell each person. Keep looking for different attributes to appreciate. Just as real estate investments appreciate in value, so will the appreciation deposits you put into your family's bank account.

1 _____

2 _____

3 _____

SPECIAL OFFER: Contact us at www.teenfrontier.com and ask for your free list of ways to show kids you care.

It's wonderful to want to have enhanced relationships as long as you don't try too hard to have a great relationship. Keep from being too attached to the outcome. People who make having good relationships a cause or a reason for living repel others. Instead of focusing on your outcome, simply impact others by being a caring person who is genuinely interested in affirming and inspiring others whenever you can.

> *"The root meaning of the word **encouragement** is **to give heart**. When we encourage our children, we give them courage from our hearts to theirs..."*
>
> Dorothy Law Nolte and Rachel Harris

You know you are making progress with affirming words when

- You prefer to endorse vs. berate
- You focus on your teen's strengths, not flaws
- You identify your teen's good points and speak to those
- You celebrate your teens achievements
- You are unconditionally constructive when you give feedback
- Your teen feels that you are sincerely appreciative of him or her
- Your teen feels inspired by your words
- Your family relationships are filled with love and joy

CHAPTER 16

#6 Supportive Communication

This chapter builds on all of the previous skills we have discussed thus far. To be truly supportive, you need to also be empathetic, open, and flexible. When your approach is kind and you are filled with love for yourself and another, you are rewarded with having closer relationships. Don't let hurt feelings get in the way. Be diligent about promptly discussing misunderstandings. To give effective support, remember to invoke gentle and insightful inquiry to learn about the situation at hand, and give thoughtful affirming words. Together these skills comprise supportive communication, helping you collaboratively discuss situations where your focus is to connect rather than to control.

Communicating in this manner is powerful because you learn to accept "what is" rather than waste time and energy in arguing, disregarding or denying what is. It could even entail letting your teen win an argument! To help yourself detach from "who's right," practice taking turns being "right." Realize each situation is what it is; you simply acknowledge the situation without reacting to it. And you find healthy ways to be collaborative, show your support, and derive enjoyment from creating positive outcomes.

Elizabeth is a single mom who with her teen moved from Denver to California where Elena began her freshman year in high school. Elena complained that her teachers had unclear expectations and that the school's mentality was stifling; there was more emphasis on disciplining than learning. Mom said that Elena had always been a bright and willing student until now. Elizabeth didn't know whether Elena was just being a difficult teenager or if her sudden lackluster performance and dislike for her new school were problems that needed further exploration. Unsure how to handle this situation, Elizabeth enrolled in one of my parent teen coaching programs. Afterwards, she realized that her daughter's complaints needed her support. Elizabeth shifted from the controlling talk of "You need to find a way to make it work" to an enhanced, supportive approach "Let's look at some options."

Mother and daughter did some research on the Internet and found a Steiner Waldorf School with an enlightened teaching style. These worldwide schools are known for their quality in education and their forward-thinking philosophy to "Accept the children with reverence, educate them with love, and send them forth in freedom." Elena began to thrive again, unlike her best friend who wasn't as fortunate to have a mother who was willing to listen, acknowledge, and collaborate; not fix, ignore or react to teen complaints.

Another parent, Sheryl, who was committed to taking into account her teen's unique needs and preferences, agreed to send her son to military school. Interestingly, Sheryl personally abhors guns and violence of any kind (her husband and son don't share that belief), but she was willing to set her agenda aside and actively supported a decision that fit with what her son wanted for his life. Parents faced with this sort of dilemma are often tempted to force their views and their vision onto kids instead of realizing that they are interfering with the life purpose of another human being. As Kahlil Gibran said in *The Prophet*, "Your children are not your children . . . they come through you but not from you... You may strive to be like them, but seek not to make them like you..." Her son was very happy and grateful to attend West Point, embarking on the future of his choice.

Another way of demonstrating supportive communication skills is by providing clear choices to your children. This skill will help you bypass much frustration. Rebecca is a career woman with two stepchildren, both teenagers. During the week, her kids are responsible for making their own breakfast. On the weekends, she enjoys cooking a big breakfast for her family. Rather than insisting that everyone have the same omelet, she offers a range of choices (ham, cheese, mushrooms, tomatoes, spinach, etc.) Taking their preferences into consideration, contributes to their connectedness. Both teens look forward to the weekend breakfasts with their parents.

Consider offering age appropriate choices early; don't wait until your children are almost young adults. Daniel, a father of a three-year-old-son, successfully provides a set of structured choices (three options) to him regularly. I'm astounded by the wise choices his son makes. Granted this child is exceptional. Another young child might feel burdened with too many choices at such a tender age. Use your intuition. The point is most parents aren't accustomed to asking themselves "What choices can I offer my child?" It seems easier to automatically replicate the traditional pattern of telling your kids what to do, or not do, without providing choices or clear consequences. Be willing to give your reasons for the guidelines you set for your teen. Saying "Because I said so" won't help your kid develop his or her own ability to reason. This parenting style stifles a child's natural expression, limits potential, and only causes a rift in your relationship. Here are some examples of controlling talk that breeds frustration and resentment:

"Do it the way I say, and don't ask me why."

"That's not what you really want."
"Wouldn't you agree that . . .?"
"Don't you think that . . .?"
"You shouldn't even let those lofty thoughts enter
your head."
"Who do you think you are?"
"What's wrong with you?"

No doubt you've heard these statements; maybe you even use some of them. Most of our parenting we learned by default from watching our parents and/or television. No wonder we frequently find ourselves in messy and drama-laden interactions. Let's take the subject of homework. Parents often complain to me that they can't get their daughter or son to do it. Nagging, commanding "Just do it," or attempting guilt "If you really wanted to get your work done, you would have finished it on time," doesn't get to the underlying issues or concerns; it just exasperates the problem.

Ralph's son claimed that he doesn't have enough time to do his homework, be at his part-time job, and do the chores he is responsible for around the house. Here's how Ralph approached this recurring situation. He asked his overwhelmed son, Mark, to share with him everything on his To Do list. Then, Ralph helped Mark prioritize his list; he asked, "What are the consequences if this doesn't get done today?" Soon it became clear that Mark didn't have to do it all today. There were only about three things that had to get done right now in order for Mark to be prepared at school, feel caught up at home, go to work, and still have time for his friends.

After asking "What might get in the way of this time management plan we've designed together," they discovered that Mark allows himself to get distracted by answering his cell phone when his friends call. Mark is committed to doing his best at his studies and has agreed to limit his phone time to when he is truly available to talk, not when he is in the middle of writing a paper for school. Mark isn't consistent yet, but he's remembering more often than not. As a parent coach,

Ralph went beyond what was said. He didn't get hooked by Mark's description of the situation. Ralph was successful in creating the type of relationship with his son that allowed for learning to take place. Mark gained self awareness and a new perception about time. He was now equipped to achieve the agreed upon goals.

Contrast this approach with the more traditional accusing statement often made by parents, "If you didn't waste all of your time talking with your friends, you'd get your work done." It sounds judgmental and closes the door to discovery and resolution. Supportive communication helps teens learn about themselves and find their own answers.

Ralph, senior level financial executive, knew from his own experience that good time management skills don't just happen; they are learned. He also understood that managing time is really about managing yourself and that if he can guide Mark now on how to do this well, Mark won't have to learn it the hard way as an adult. Plus, his son will be able to make much better choices going forward, based on what's really important to him, rather than stressing about not being able to have it all.

Supportive communication helps teens to discover for themselves new thoughts and feelings. Frederic, a vice president in the oil industry, got caught in a corporate reorganization and lost his job. He was fortunate that it only took him 30 days to locate a new position. The family was relieved that he found a great new opportunity, but reluctant to leave Colorado and move further west.

Daughter Mari in particular, a freshman in high school, had strong resistance to the sudden change. Frederic asked her, "What is the hardest thing about this change for you?" Mari was mostly concerned about losing her friends. He acknowledged that and then asked, "What's the scariest part of the change for you?" This question revealed that she was afraid of not having the support of close friends during her high school years, that there wouldn't be anyone she could relate to. "How realistic is this fear?" "What happens if you stay stuck in this fear?" "What could you do about it?" Mari admitted that she made friends easily and that certainly there would be someone in school or in the youth program at church that she could befriend.

Notice that your role as parent coach is not to fix the situation, but to help your teen dialogue about it. This empowers them to find their own solutions with you as their guide. In this instance, Mari's feelings were lovingly acknowledged first, so that she could then shift into looking at the opportunities contained within this change: She could start over and reinvent herself. She could learn about another part of the U.S., and so on. As it turned out, her family moved to a larger, new house with a swimming pool. Soon Mari's biggest decisions focused on which friends to invite to her pool party.

Exercise

A. Look for opportunities to be supportive today. Be extra alert for how you can be kind to yourself and your teen. When you can think about yourself compassionately and take time out for yourself, it will be much easier to be there for your loved ones.

B. Respectful support needs to be given on an individual basis, not on how you were parented or what worked with your oldest child. One size does not fit all. If you have more than one child, take into account the unique needs, interests, temperament, and goals of each one. I often say, "A fish sees water last." Water is a given. It's difficult to see ourselves clearly; we all have blinders. So, to find out how well you are doing, get feedback from your teen. Ask the following:

1. In your view, what would improve our relationship?

2. What kind of support would you like from me/us?

3. What is one thing that you want me to stop doing and/or start doing?

Sometimes it takes several sincere attempts before your teen will take you seriously and trust that you really want the answers to these questions. Don't give up. Wait a while and then invite your teen's feedback again at another time. Most teens will appreciate your effort to learn new ways to parent and communicate.

In this chapter, you have learned that supportive communication means taking the time to draw out, listen with empathy, ask questions that cause your teen to think, and help your teen come to important realizations that allow for new possibilities to surface. In addition, being supportive means that you honor your teen's need to remain silent and work out his or her own thoughts first before sharing them with you. Pressuring someone because you are ready to talk is not respectful. Let your teen know that you're available; keep the door open.

You know you are making progress with supportive communication when

- You respond with comments that fully relate to what is being said
- You stay focused on your teen's goals, problem or situation
- You solicit feedback from your teen
- You provide a clear set of choices
- You are willing to explore options
- You respect your teen's need for silence
- You use a collaborative approach with your teen
- You accept "what is" without wishing it were different
- Your support allows your teen to stop and think with effective tools to make it worthwhile

CHAPTER 17

#7 Facilitating Growth

Most parents would agree that a key function of parenting is to prepare your teen for self-determining, responsible, and accountable behavior. We want our kids to be fully functioning and contributing adults within the family and within society. To this end, teenagers are naturally programmed to seek their self-identity and yearn for independence so that they can develop into adulthood. During this time, teenagers start to withdraw from their parents and experience fluctuating moods. Did you know that the word adolescence means "breaking away?" Often parents have mixed feelings about a teen's drive for independence. On the one hand, you can't wait for them to graduate and be on their own; and on the other, you have trouble letting go of your babies. In this chapter, you will learn how to facilitate growth and learning; thus, finding a balance between maintaining a healthy heart connection and fostering self-reliance.

Here is a summary of typical ways that the inherent desire for independence and self-identity is expressed by teens (or preteens):

- They prefer spending time with their friends instead of with the family

- They insist on having their own private room and the freedom to decorate as they please

- They begin to choose which thoughts and feelings they want to share with you

- They request that you honor their personal property

- They listen to music that is different from what you enjoy

- They use language and phrases that you don't understand

- They wear clothes and accessories that clearly identify their teenage culture

- They question your values and beliefs

I recommend that whenever possible, it's best to be flexible and comply with your teen's needs for physical, emotional, mental, and spiritual space. You will want to draw on all the previous coaching skills in this book to help you during this critical stage of development. Without practice, parents tend to get defensive when the teen complains "You have no right to move or take any of my personal things from my room." A typical response by parents is, "If you would keep your room clean, I wouldn't have to go in your room and clean it." Initially, I too, made this mistake, and learned from it. Parents who are unwilling to let go of their old parenting habits will become estranged and miss their opportunity to guide their teens into becoming responsible and contributing adults.

Underlying most of the conflicts between parents and teens is the confusion about whose responsibility it is to govern the teen. If you believe that it's the parent's right to decide what teenagers are to do and believe, and you push your views onto your offspring, then your relationship will become adversarial. Remember, it's the teenager's job to seek independence. Parent coaches understand that teens need to be free to think independently, have meaningful dialogue with you, check in with their own inner knowing, and take responsibility for their choices. Otherwise, you will rob your children of valuable learning experiences. Growth then will be inhibited, not facilitated.

Okay, many of you probably want to know, "What am I responsible for?" Your responsibility is to help your kids to take self responsibility. If responsibility is the left hand, then independence (freedom) is the right hand; together there is equilibrium. Kids need your help to understand the relationship between these principles.

In our world, an adult has the freedom (independence) to buy a car, but we need to pay for it or get financing (responsibility). We have the freedom to gain employment, but we need to show up for work and meet certain standards. We have the privilege of traveling to foreign countries, but we must have a valid passport, and so on. Wise parents realize that they can best prepare their kids for adulthood by providing boundaries that link independence with responsibility.

For example, if you decide to gift your teen with a car (independence to drive off on their own) be sure to outline the responsibilities that go along with this new possession. Ron, father of a 16-year-old daughter, required Alexa to take a locally offered class on car maintenance before he provided her with a used Subaru. As a result, Alexa, became skilled at basic maintenance procedures and could swiftly change a flat tire. Having this knowledge gave Alexa greater confidence in herself. She knew that she could handle being on the road by herself. Alexa had a part-time job and paid for her own gasoline. Some parents wait until their teens go to college (or beyond!) before they ask their son or daughter to handle this responsibility. There are no hard and fast rules about when to include financial responsibilities. And yet, why not start early and take incremental steps toward giving more independence and responsibility as your teen matures? If you pay for the gasoline, then you can limit how often your teen has access to the car; or you can provide a tank of gas per week, and anything beyond that is the responsibility of your kid.

If your teen doesn't have a job yet, consider having him or her commit to allocating a portion of their regular allowance for car expenses. Helping your teen understand how to allocate money now will be important for handling a household budget in the future. Be clear about what expenses the teenager is responsible for. This approach is much more empowering than having to ask mom or dad for some money every other day. Teens can't learn to manage money if they don't have any, and can't learn to manage money if you always pay for everything. Help your teen list expenditures and demonstrate budgeting.

Some parents, thrilled to be relieved of chauffeuring, are reluctant to have their teens share expenses and would rather pay for all of it. Others still treat their teens as children and continue to do everything (laundry, cooking, managing their finances, etc.) for them. Do you really want to continue being a caretaker or would you rather help kids become self-reliant? If you don't teach them these basic life skills and provide practice opportunities, who will? Opportunities, not obligations, promote learning.

The bottom line is that parents who start linking independence with responsibility early see a marked difference in healthy self-esteem and self-reliance. Teenagers without such opportunities often develop an entitlement mentality that can follow them into adulthood. How will your decisions about giving freedom balanced with responsibility help your teen in college, on the job or in other life situations? Ask yourself, "How am I preparing my teen for life?" "Are my actions in alignment with my goals?"

Parents are also responsible for setting reasonable boundaries (rules) and consequences with the teenager to ensure that agreements are honored. As a maturing young adult, it's high time to include your teen in both, if you haven't done so already. If the rule and the corresponding consequences are discussed together up front, it won't feel arbitrary and there won't be any surprises. Think about it. Do you know what the consequences are if your payment to a credit card company is late? Of course, you do. Credit card companies furnish this information to you. They don't arbitrarily arrive at a late fee after the fact. If you don't agree with the consequence, you have the freedom to choose another company with a longer grace period or a lower late fee or choose to abstain from using credit cards.

Martha's visiting 13-year-old stepdaughter, Vanessa, wanted to make tacos for the family all by herself. Martha agreed to give Vanessa free reign in the kitchen and asked her whether she would take responsibility for making sure the kitchen was clean before they all left the house to head to the movie theater. No problem. Vanessa was eager to get started and shooed Martha out of the kitchen. The taco dinner turned out great. The family praised Vanessa's cooking and placed their plates in the dishwasher, leaving only a few cooking utensils, counters, and the stove for her to clean up.

When Martha returned to the kitchen to see how Vanessa was doing, she was no where to be seen and the stove and counters were still a mess. Martha found Vanessa in her room and when she asked about the kitchen, Vanessa said she would clean up after they all returned home from their movie outing. Martha reminded her that the agreement they made was for Vanessa to complete her clean up before the outing, not afterwards. Martha was disappointed and upset, but collected herself and calmly replied that Vanessa had a choice. She could still take responsibility for cleaning the kitchen right now and go to the cinema with the family, or she could stay home, miss out on seeing the movie, and leisurely clean up the kitchen. Vanessa was unprepared for this consequence, but quickly recovered and chose to get the kitchen clean in the next 10 minutes.

In this example, Martha understood that it was important to teach her stepdaughter to honor agreements and that there needed to be a reasonable consequence. Martha also intuitively knew that providing Vanessa with a choice instead of an edict was likely to result in a positive outcome. An even better approach would have been to give

Vanessa a voice in sharing her ideas about possible consequences upfront rather than waiting until the agreement was violated and then pronouncing the consequence. Predetermined consequences prevent the parent from overreacting; thus, by-passing potential drama between both the parent and the teen. Furthermore without predetermined consequences in place, inconsistencies result. We are all influenced by our feelings. When parents are in a good mood, they are inclined to overlook infractions. When parents are in a bad mood, they react and often respond aggressively. Inconsistencies create confusion and resentment. As a parent coach you can help bring forward points of view that are in alignment with your teen's goals. Let's say your teen is filled with ideas for a possible career choice but lacks the clarity to bring them to completion. You have already done the first three parent coaching steps and now you begin asking insightful questions that explore which ideas create the most energy passion and excitement for you teen. Ask which strengths, talents, and interests will be highlighted for each option. After engaging your teen in this type of conversation, ask how he or she might use these insights for making decisions that will help forward the action, to take the next step.

Jen's exploratory conversation with her son, Aaron, resulted in her 17-year-old realizing that his talent and passion lie in combining computer technology and cars. Aaron imagined that he would be most fulfilled if he could repair the sophisticated computer circuitry found in luxury automobiles. Jen provided immediate support and facilitated growth by asking what next step Aaron could take now to locate this specialized training. Aaron committed to doing the research and quickly found schools in New Mexico and Utah. Jen understood that Aaron had both the freedom and the responsibility to decide about his future vocation.

Without parent coach training, many parents find it difficult to adequately help their teens make good choices because they have trouble themselves. Good decision-making is rarely addressed in schools and overlooked in parenting. How do you make choices? Do you trust your ability to choose well? Most of us have never been taught to make wise decisions in our work or personal life. If this applies to you, take a look at the top eight ways to make great choices in Appendix 5. Practice making deliberate choices so that you can be a great role model and guide.

Without knowing how to make good choices, long-term goals usually give way to immediate gratification. It's easier to watch a show on TV than to do homework. It's easier to skip class on a beautiful spring day than to listen and learn. It's easier to apply at a college where you're virtually guaranteed entry than to have the courage to get into a highly reputable university (that can open many more doors of opportunity). The world is filled with people whose life and career choices do not support their highest vision of themselves because they settled for easier choices with short-term results.

Exercise

A. Learning to balance independence and responsibility is a big step for many teens. Begin identifying an area of responsibility where you would like to facilitate growth. Ask yourself the following questions to help you clarify what you want to request of your teen.

What do I hope to accomplish by making this request?

_____

_____

How will it serve my teen?

_____

_____

Who will be responsible for what?

_____

_____

What are my specific expectations (standards, quality, time frame or behaviors)?

_____

_____

_____

What are the check points or milestones for this area of responsibility?

_____

_____

What information can I provide or demonstrate to facilitate growth or success?

_____

_____

_____

How can I affirm and support my teen during this process?

_____

_____

What consequences do we need to discuss in advance in case the ball gets dropped?

_____

_____

_____

B. Now that you have thought through the above questions, schedule a meeting with your teen. Say something like, "I/we have observed that you are showing more signs of being able to make good decisions, and that I/we want to foster your independence tempered with responsibility. Soon you will be an adult, and you'll be fully responsible for your actions and your life. I/we are very excited for you and want to support you as you face the many changes ahead. Much can be learned now while you are still a teenager. So, let's together take a look at some options that will give you plenty of opportunity to practice being self-reliant. I/we want to help you better prepare for your future."

_____

_____

_____

Next discuss your specific ideas and get input from your teen (using all of the skills you have been practicing thus far). Make sure your agreements are clear and check for understanding. Ask your teen, in his or her own words, to describe what he or she will now be responsible for and outline the steps that need to be taken to get the agreed-upon results.

_____

_____

Record your clear agreement here:

_____

_____

C. To assist you in developing your new seven coaching skills, begin using the checklist below. (You'll find it again in Appendix 6.)

7 Parent Coach Questions Checklist

Use the following checklist as an aid to remember this 7-step approach. I suggest you make additional copies for yourself and keep them handy.

Heart Connection
1. Am I feeling centered and focusing on a positive outcome?

Coaching Presence
2. Am I fully present, open, and alert?

Conscious Listening
3. Am I listening to learn rather than thinking about my next response?

Insightful Questioning
4. Am I asking questions that clarify and generate meaningful dialogue?

Affirming Words
5. Am I frequently validating or expressing appreciation?

Supportive Communication
6. Am I focused on the talker's agenda and responding to what was said?

Facilitating Growth
7. Am I allowing learning to take place and promoting self-responsibility?

SELF OBSERVATION/NOTES

What do I want to do more of?

_____

What do I want to do less of?

_____

What will I do differently next time?

_____

Congratulations on completing the Seven Simple Steps to help you *Coach Your Teen to Success!* You are well on your way to transforming your important relationships. Know that the more you practice, the more proficient you will become.

In summary, a parent coach stays in the background while keeping focused on the teen to best facilitate growth and progress, leading from behind instead of from the front. On the surface, it appears that the actions of the coach go largely unnoticed. Since the coach doesn't dictate, push or control, there is no resistance. Coaching sessions flow smoothly. There is great appreciation for the parent coach because the coach supports the young adult's agenda, rather than promoting his or her own. A full range of topics are encouraged and since the coach is not attached to a particular outcome, there is no need to argue or manipulate. There is pure openness, receptivity, and support. Permission is given to fail to ensure that success is accelerated.

*"A leader is best when people barely know he exists,
not so good when people obey and acclaim him, worse when
they despise him . . . But of a good leader who talks little
when his work is done, his aim fulfilled, they will say, "We did
it ourselves."*

Lao-Tzu (Founder of Taoism)

You know you are making progress with facilitating growth when

- You are flexible in helping your teen explore his or her specific needs for self-identity and independence

- You encourage your teen to think independently from you and make his or her own choices

- You enjoy brainstorming and assist in helping your teen define actions that serve to provide deep learning

- You make clear requests and arrive at specific agreements that include consequences

- You demonstrate and facilitate good decision-making strategies

- You celebrate your teen's milestones and capabilities for future growth.

- Your interventions are gentle ("less is more")

- You have let go and are at peace with yourself

EPILOGUE

Bravo! You are well on your way to open, heal, and enhance your parent-teen relationships; thus, positively impacting this current generation and future generations. It's been my observation in coaching parents, teens, and other caring adults that with a sincere commitment to consistently apply this 7-step approach, there are no shortages of success stories. With daily practice you will evolve from "doing coaching" to "becoming a coach." When this occurs, being a coach will be synonymous with who you are. Helping teens find their own success will be second nature. Sharing success with others is great fun, highly rewarding, and benefits everyone.

The biggest stumbling block you'll run into relates to the need to be in control. The more you are willing to let go of control, the more effortless your progress will be. Do you really feel more secure or safe when you attempt to control your time, reputation, relationships, children, employees, events, results or other people's opinions? How well has it been working for you? Have you ever been able to change someone's opinion when they aren't willing? How do you feel when things don't go according to your plan? Do you experience anxiety or peace of mind? Notice that when you don't insist on having specific expectations, you cannot be disappointed, and you bypass stress.

All that yanking, pushing, and forcing rarely gives us what we want. And if by chance it does, at what cost? Forcing another to do what you think is right, does not lead toward learning or self-responsibility. Rather it leads to defiance and resistance. On the surface, it might appear that an individual is compliant to your wishes, but inwardly resentment grows. How do you feel about an authority figure's interference in your life? Does your respect for this person increase or diminish? Do you get defensive or disappear? How does it impact your degree of confidence in yourself? What do you think would happen if you allowed yourself to let go of control? Do you think you would be worse off?

Those who push think they are successfully moving ahead, when in fact they are only creating obstacles. It's a paradox. The more force you use, the more it will backfire. The more you let go, the greater your chances of getting the results you want. Have you ever tried to force your key into a lock and then when you relaxed your grip, it worked like a charm? When you relax with the intention to join forces, rather than fight it, life becomes easier and less stressful. Letting go of control doesn't mean you stop doing or caring. It means you care enough to offer gentle facilitations instead of harsh ones. Imagine making a tight fist with your hands. How easily can you give to others or receive when your hands are clenched? Now open your fists and feel the difference. When you are in an open and relaxed state, you can connect with your inner intelligence and allow life to unfold naturally.

People resort to controlling behavior when they fear the unknown. Not knowing what to expect can be delightful instead of frightening. What if you could know in advance what was going to happen every minute of the day? How long would it be before you would be completely bored? Given the choice, isn't it a lot more interesting when you don't know what to expect? What could you do to get more comfortable with the unknown?

When you believe that you need something outside of yourself to feel secure, you will be dependent on others and continue to struggle. Conversely, when you are secure within and trust yourself to handle any situation that crops up, you are free. You will no longer link your wellbeing to another person's behavior. With this level of personal power, you can easily let others make their own choices. How do you reconnect to your resourceful and confident self? With love. Love is all you need to get grounded, feel secure, and let go of control. The next time you feel tempted to pull on the reigns of control, ask yourself, "What's my motivation? What's the fear behind my motivation?" Are you allowing the presence of love or are you being faithful to fear?

Love intervenes gently.	Fear intervenes harshly.
Love allows for self-determination.	Fear commands.
Love is open and attentive.	Fear obstructs and ignores.
Love tells the truth.	Fear denies and withholds.
Love is patient.	Fear wants it immediately.
Love listens to learn.	Fear controls the conversation.
Love admits mistakes.	Fear insists on being right.

To benefit from the healing power of love, acknowledge your fears. These pseudo fears don't protect, they prevent the presence of love. As you return to love, you will wear your personal power lightly, walk with impeccability, approach others with compassion, live up to the highest vision of yourself, and inspire your children to realize their potential.

APPENDIX 1

Teen Suicide Prevention Tips

Nearly every hour another young adult commits suicide.

When my daughter was 13, she lost her best friend to suicide. Everyone affected was devastated at the loss of this young life. In addition to the confusion and the grief, there was guilt, "If only I could have done something differently to prevent it." If you are like I was, you probably don't know much about suicide—but I do now.

Why did Leslie (we'll call her that) do it? We can only speculate. Why does anyone commit suicide? It's when problems seem insurmountable and you feel there is no where to turn. According to the American Academy of Pediatrics (www.aap.org, 2004), "Young people reported that when they tried to tell their parents about their feelings of unhappiness their mother and father denied or ignored their point of view." **In using the 7 Simple Steps** you will know how to break through your teen's sense of isolation; a critical key in preventing teen suicide.

- Reassure your teen that you are willing to listen without letting your emotions get in the way
- Ask about feelings and acknowledge them even if none of it makes sense to you (don't lecture or dismiss his or her reasons)
- Provide loving support; this includes seeking professional help.

APPENDIX 2

ADD/ADHD Books and Resources

1. *No More Ritalin: Treating ADHD Without Drugs*, by Mary Ann Block, D.O. New York, NY: Kensington Publishing Corp., 1996.

   Written by a mother who became a physician to help her child, this book provides an easy-to-understand overview of the history of ADD/ADHD, how it is diagnosed, and outlines current treatments. It includes an effective alternate treatment based on Osteopathic Philosophy.

2. *Running on Ritalin: A Physician Reflects on Children, Society, and Performance on a Pill*, by Lawrence H. Diller, M.D. New York, NY: Bantam Books, 1998.

   Written from a medical perspective, Dr. Diller's book provides in-depth information on ADD/ADHD. This book is top-notch and a must read if your child is using Ritalin. You can also go to Dr. Diller's web site at www.docdiller.com where you'll find excerpts from the book, papers on Ritalin, and related topics.

3. *The Ritalin Fact Book*, by Peter R. Breggin, M.D., Cambridge, MA: Perseus Books Group, 2002.

Dr. Breggin has written several books on Ritalin. He is a psychiatrist, parent, Harvard educated, and founder of the International Center for the Study of Psychiatry and Psychology. Breggin believes that "ADHD is a controversial diagnosis with little or no scientific or medical basis." He gave testimony on the adverse effects of Ritalin and related drugs before the Subcommittee on Oversight and Investigations in the U.S. House of Representatives. For more information, you can visit his site at www.breggin.com.

ADD-Friendly Organization:

C.H.A.D.D.: Adults and Children with Attention-Deficit/Hyperactive Disorder; A national resource for AD/HD. www.chadd.org or call 800-233-4050 (Landover, MD).

APPENDIX 3

Parenting Styles Answer Key

1. a=2, b=3, c=1
2. a=1, b=2, c=3
3. a=2, b=3, c=1
4. a=1, b=2, c=3
5. a=3, b=1, c=2
6. a=1, b=2, c=3
7. a=2, b=1, c=3
8. a=3, b=1, c=2
9. a=2, b=3, c=1

10. a=1, b=3, c=2
11. a=1, b=3, c=2
12. a=2, b=3, c=1
13. a=1, b=3, c=2
14. a=2, b=1, c=3
15. a=2, b=1, c=3
16. a=1, b=2, c=3
17. a=3, b=1, c=2
18. a=1, b=2, c=3

APPENDIX 4

Seven Conversation Deepeners

A coaching trademark is to ask powerful questions. To generate more meaningful discussions with your preteens or teens, the questions below will get you started and/or feel free to craft your own. Just remember there are no wrong answers and be sure to give your kid plenty of time to answer. Don't assume your teen wants to know how you would answer. Check in first. Have fun with this.

1. Imagine you've graduated from high school (or college). What kind of memories or experiences do you want to take with you? What's important to you about_____ (each one)?

2. If you could produce a movie, what would the title (or plot) be? Which actors would you select to star in it?

3. What do you imagine it would be like to live in (pick a foreign country)? What might be the same/different? Which country (or countries) are you curious about?

4. Which natural talents of yours do you enjoy the most? (Note: talent is defined as a natural ability, aptitude or recurring productive behavior.)

5. What are some of your recurring fears? What are some of your happiest moments?

6. If our roles were reversed and you were my parent (aunt, grandparent, etc.), what would you do differently?

7. What do you like about yourself the most? What trait or quality would you like others to recognize in you?

APPENDIX 5

Top Eight Ways to Make Great Decisions

1. What are my options?

    Asking this question puts you in a resourceful state. If you can only arrive at two options, know that you are limiting yourself. Most people choose between option A or B. Keep going until you have three options. Five is better! If you hear yourself saying, "I have no options," recognize that you are simply not aware of them yet. Expand your options by gathering information, talking with others or working with a coach.

2. Take each option and ask, "Then what would probably happen?"

    Be strategic. Take your top three options and use your imagination to focus in great detail on what would happen if you acted on this choice. See what unfolds and feel the impact as if you have already experienced this selection. Take it well into the future by asking, "Then what?" at least two more times. Take time to be aware of the worst-case and best-case scenarios. What would you do in each case? How would that be for you? The result of even one choice has a domino effect on ourselves and others. Our lives are shaped by our choices every day.

3. How does this decision fit with me, my values, and my purpose?

   For example, if integrity is important to you, you could ask yourself, "Does this choice I'm about to make cause me to make a deposit into my personal integrity account?" Check for congruence between what you say you believe and what you actually do. Being clear about who you are and what is important for you allows you to make better decisions.

4. Am I trusting my intuition?

   Your intuition is your personal guide to help you sense what is right for you. To access it, determine how you feel about the decision. Be sure to check in with your heart, not your gut. Research by the HeartMath Institute indicates that the true seat of the mind is in the heart. I recommend that you practice using your intuition on minor decisions to build your confidence in intimately knowing how your intuition shows up for you. It's important for you to be able to distinguish between fear and intuition. Access a memory from the past when you made a successful decision and remember how that felt.

5. Am I setting my ego aside and listening to my Higher Power?

   By accessing your intuition, you are tapping into your inner wisdom. For further guidance, especially for critical decisions, consider going beyond yourself to make sure your ego-mind isn't interfering. This step is a very personal one. You will know how best to do this. Some people pray, dream, meditate or commune with nature. Be sure to listen long enough to hear your answers.

6. What would I do if I were bolder (notice that I didn't say "reckless")?

   Look at your life to see if you settle rather than focus on what you really want. Be willing to negotiate. One of my mottos is, "If you don't ask, you don't get!" Many people have an internal thermostat that causes them to cool down whenever they go beyond their comfort zone. Do you find that you stop at a certain level of success? Remember, there is no failure, only feedback.

7. Do I really expect a positive outcome?

   Where is your focus? If your orientation is negative and you worry about the outcome, you will be giving energy to what you don't want to happen. This is how we unwittingly sabotage our own success. Often we do this because of erroneously thinking that we are protecting ourselves from disappointment and pain should things not turn out to our liking. Once you are this far along in the decision-making process, you are much better off acting as if your desired outcome is already assured.

8. What regrets will I have about my choice?

   This question can relate to missed opportunities or to regrets stemming from integrity glitches. Be willing to look at the pattern of your past choices. These choices mirror (to yourself and others) your true personal thoughts and feelings—that is, how you really view yourself and the world. A litmus test for some people is, "How does this choice fit with what I'm teaching my children (or those I care about)?" Identify limiting beliefs that are getting in the way of your making great choices. If you are not able to clearly see your patterns, ask a trusted friend or get a qualified coach to help you.

APPENDIX 6

Seven Parent Coach Questions Checklist

Use this checklist to remember the Seven Simple Steps.

Heart Connection
1. Am I feeling centered and focusing on a positive outcome?

Coaching Presence
2. Am I fully present, open, and alert?

Conscious Listening
3. Am I listening to learn rather than thinking about my next response?

Insightful Questioning

4. Am I asking questions that clarify and generate meaningful dialogue?

Affirming Words

5. Am I frequently validating or expressing appreciation?

Supportive Communication

6. Am I focused on the talker's agenda and responding to what was said?

Facilitating Growth

7. Am I allowing learning to take place and promoting self-responsibility?

SELF OBSERVATION/NOTES

What do I want to do more of?

_____

What do I want to do less of?

_____

What will I do differently next time?

_____

Congratulations! You are well on your way to transforming your important relationships. Know that the more you practice, the more proficient you will become.

APPENDIX 7

Form Your Own Teen Frontier Community

Wouldn't it be great to meet with a small group of parents who are serious about learning and practicing parent-teen coaching skills? Imagine how much positive support you could offer each other. You'll strengthen your resolve and courage to apply the Seven Simple Steps contained in this book when you invite others to join you. Here are some tips to make it a successful group experience:

1. The most effective groups have 6-8 members. (Get started as soon as you have one other member and other members will follow.)

2. Meet on the same day and at the same time each week (or biweekly) to ensure good attendance and to build connection within your community.

3. Ask members to commit to attending for at least three months to increase your level of success.

4. Establish your purpose and group guidelines upfront (instill confidentiality, give equal time for speaking, limit unsolicited advice, acknowledge each member, stay focused on the chapters in this book, and be respectful).

5. Rotate experienced facilitators when possible.

6. Ask members to commit to taking specific action prior to the next meeting.

7. Allow each member to ask for additional support (resource information, phone support, etc.).

8. Periodically solicit feedback from the group to find out what is working and what isn't working.

[For more information on how to get started, register at www.teenfrontier.com.]

About the Author

Barbara McRae, MCC, is a parent and founder of Teen Frontier International, a division of EnhancedLife Coaching, LLC®. She holds the highest coaching distinction earned through the International Coach Federation—the gold medal standard in coaching. Barbara is a recognized expert in professional coaching as profiled in *Business Week* magazine, *USA Today*, and *The New York Times*, and elsewhere. As a Certified Hypnotherapist, she assists clients in the elimination of limiting beliefs and the discovery of powerful internal resources. McRae has transformed the lives of thousands of individuals, both adults and teens. Ninety percent of Barbara's work is accomplished over the telephone worldwide (1:1 coaching, group coaching, and teleclasses). She is a published self-improvement author and a motivational speaker. As an experienced Big Sister and an active board member of Big Brothers Big Sisters of Colorado, Inc., she is dedicated to mentoring present day preteens and teens.

An artist and poet, Barbara and her husband live in Colorado. Visit Barbara at www.teenfrontier.com.

Dear Reader,

I hope you have found *Coach Your Teen to Success* valuable. In the spirit of coaching, I'd love your feedback. Please answer the following questions or use your own format.

1. What helped me the most?
2. What did I have the greatest difficulty with?
3. How did I overcome the above challenge?
4. What other topics would I like help with?
5. What else would I like you to know?

Please give us your feedback by registering at www.teenfrontier.com (or call us at 888-409-5433) and let me know if we have your permission to reprint your feedback in promotional material for *Coach Your Teen to Success* or in future publications.

Thank you for taking the time to share your thoughts. I wish you life-long success!

All the best,

Barbara McRae, MCC
Teen Frontier International

Additional Ways You Can Participate with Barbara McRae and Teen Frontier International

- Personal one-on-one telecoaching

- Group telecoaching

- Workshops

- Book Barbara to speak at your organization

OR become a provider of
Coach Your Teen to Success™

call 1-888-409-5433.

If you are a professional coach, teacher, counselor, therapist, social worker or if you provide educational programs to parents or mentors, contact us about how you can deliver our Coach Your Teen To Success™ program. It's a wonderful way for you to expand your current menu of services, impact generation and after generation, and add a new source of revenue.

To obtain FREE tips, articles, and updates on parent coach topics, as they are published, visit us at:

www.TeenFrontier.com

Bulk orders of *Coach Your Teen to Success* are also available!

NOTES